COST ACCOUNTING

About the Authors

Michael R. Skigen received his B.S.B.A. from Lehigh University and his M.B.A. from New York University, where he was a Ford Foundation Doctoral Workshop Fellow. He is Associate Professor, School of Business Administration, Georgetown University in Washington, D. C., and a certified public accountant in Maryland. He previously taught at George Washington University and at Pace College, and was a financial analyst and accountant at Humble Oil and Standard Oil Company (N.J.). Professor Skigen is coauthor with Professor Snyder of *A Practical Guide to Income Taxes* and has contributed articles to a number of business publications. He received the Lybrand Gold Medal for the outstanding accounting article in 1973–1974 from the National Association of Accountants.

Eugene K. Snyder received his B.A. degree from Wayne State University and his J.D. degree (with distinction) from the University of Michigan Law School. He is Assistant Vice-President–Finance at the Securities Investor Protection Corporation. He was Professor, School of Business Administration, Georgetown University, and served as Dean from 1969 to 1972. Mr. Snyder is a certified public accountant and a member of the bar in Michigan, Ohio, and the District of Columbia. He has been Controller and a Director at the Ohio Steel Foundry Company, Assistant Controller at Mechanical Handling Systems, Inc., and an instructor in accounting at the University of Detroit. Besides being coauthor of *A Practical Guide to Income Taxes*, he has written a number of articles for professional publications.

COST
ACCOUNTING

Michael R. Skigen

Eugene K. Snyder

BARNES & NOBLE BOOKS

A DIVISION OF HARPER & ROW, PUBLISHERS

New York, Hagerstown, San Francisco, London

COST ACCOUNTING. Copyright © 1975 by Michael R. Skigen and Eugene K. Snyder. All rights reserved. Printed in the United States of America. No part of this book may be used or reproduced in any manner without written permission except in the case of brief quotations embodied in critical articles and reviews. For information address Harper & Row, Publishers, Inc., 10 East 53d Street, New York, N. Y. 10022. Published simultaneously in Canada by Fitzhenry & Whiteside Limited, Toronto.

First BARNES & NOBLE BOOKS edition published 1975

LIBRARY OF CONGRESS CATALOG CARD NUMBER: 74–21723

STANDARD BOOK NUMBER: 06–460159–5

83 84 85 86   10 9 8 7

Dedicated to Rosalind, Keith, Eric, Stacey,
Ann, Ken, Rose, Bob, Mary, and John
for whose costs we are still accounting.

Contents

Preface

This outline is a compact summary of the principles of cost accounting. It can be used by the student in conjunction with standard texts to facilitate study and review. It can also be used by accountants, bookkeepers, and other business and professional people as a ready source book of cost accounting fundamentals and procedures. The material is presented as simply and concisely as possible, with a minimum of jargon.

We wish to thank our families for their forbearance while we worked, our colleagues at Georgetown University for their assistance, and particularly Jeanne Flagg, editor, Barnes & Noble Books, for her many helpful suggestions.

M.R.S.

E.K.S.

COST ACCOUNTING

CHAPTER 1

The Nature and Role of Cost Accounting

Cost accounting is central to modern management theory and practice. In two of the three basic elements of management, *planning* and *controlling*, the cost accountant's role is crucial. In the third basic element, *organizing*, recognition of the need for cost accounting and appreciation of its functions often result in a more logical and workable structure, particularly in the areas of manufacturing and distribution. Before taking up the technical material that is the subject of this book, we should first examine the role of cost accounting in relation to the remainder of the business enterprise.

MODERN MANAGEMENT THEORIES

Some theories of management take the position that the management of one enterprise is substantially like the management of another because the only skills necessary are in management per se. Other theories contend that the manager must also be highly skilled in some technical discipline such as accounting, production, engineering, or marketing. All theories agree, however, that the manager's work consists primarily in planning, organizing, and controlling.

Planning. The essential function of management is to plan. Before there can be a plan, there must be objectives. Depending on their positions in the corporate hierarchy, managers will have different objectives in mind. For example, the chief executive may be concerned with the fact that his firm is heavily dependent on Brand X. His objective in planning to change the product mix would be to reduce the dependency on Brand X. The vice-president for sales may, at the same time, be planning to increase sales of Brand X by 10 percent. His objective might be to increase market penetration. The foreman of Department 36 may well be planning on a new configuration of machinery with the objective of increasing the production and lowering the cost of a component of Brand X.

These objectives and the planning for them may or may not be inconsistent. The various objectives are coordinated by a master plan of operations known as the *budget*. (The budget and the budgetary process are discussed in depth in chapter 9.) Inasmuch as the cost accountant habitually works with the data, the very essence of the budget, his role in budget preparation is of primary importance. This is particularly true because he is one of the few staff men who works with data from all departments.

Organizing. Most organizations of any size prepare an organizational chart setting forth the relationships among individual functions within the organization. There are probably at least as many different organizational charts as there are organizations. This subject is properly dealt with in a book on management; here we will show only a schematic diagram for the organization of a hypothetical corporation (Figure 1.1).

Depending on the scale of operations, there can be expansion or contraction of the following chart as circumstances or choice makes desirable. Each of the operating or staff divisions in turn

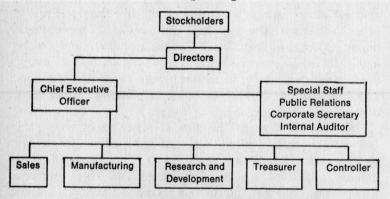

Figure 1.1. Organization of a hypothetical corporation

is subdivided as size and local conditions dictate. A particularly difficult problem arises where the company is large enough to have several divisions. The schematic diagram presented in Figure 1.1 may well be duplicated to a degree in each division. The difficult problem is posed by the situation in which the division manager reports to the executive in charge of manufacturing. Should the controller of that division report to the division manager or to the corporate controller? The mere statement of this problem illustrates why one school of management theory places a major emphasis on the role of human relations and motivation. In both theory and practice there is no definitive or "best" answer to the question. In fact, some of the largest corporations shift from one method of reporting to the other every few years and then back again.

Controlling. The cost accountant plays his major role in the control of operations. Planning and organizing in themselves, while necessary to the attainment of objectives, are not enough. There must be a system that will measure performance against plans and feed back information for future planning. Such a system is called a control system and appears as a running critique of operations. It is shown schematically in Figures 1.2 and 1.3.

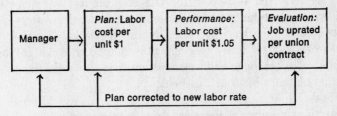

Figure 1.2. Evaluation requiring new plan

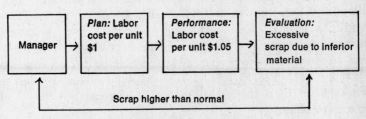

Figure 1.3. Evaluation requiring control under old plan

Two things should be apparent from the foregoing. First, the information furnished by the cost accountant is important in daily operations. Speed in reporting is therefore essential. Second, the cost accountant can do a great deal of harm with incorrect information. An analogy from the field of data processing is expressed in the acronym GIGO (garbage-in, garbage-out). Nowhere is this more relevant than in the reports of the cost accountant.

The essential element in control is that significant variations from the plan be reported as soon as possible to the responsible manager. The cost accountant's function is to analyze and report so the manager can "manage by exception." (Standard costs, the subject of chapter 10, is an essential tool in reporting variations.) Were the cost accountant permitted or required to take the action indicated by the exception, no doubt there would soon be a clash of personalities and confusion as to authority.

ROLE OF THE ACCOUNTANT IN THE FIRM

Many of the reports and analyses prepared by accountants are for use only within the firm; others, for use both within and outside the firm. Those outside the corporation for whom the accountant does his work are primarily creditors, investors, and government. This work is generally called *financial accounting*. The work that primarily concerns the operations of the corporation is called *management accounting*; it is the most important portion of the subject of this book.

Financial Accounting. Since there are as many different organizational formats as there are firms, it is impossible to do more than generalize on the two main divisions of accounting within the firm. There can be no division of accounting responsibility until the firm is of sufficient size to warrant two competent accounting executives. In general, the breakdown is between the treasury function (financial) and the controller function (managerial). (See Figure 1.1.) There is no reason for one to rank higher than the other; both should report to the chief executive officer.

The treasury function is involved with financing, credits and collections, and investment management among others and is therefore substantially removed from the day-to-day operations of the firm. This does not imply, however, that the function is merely historic. Credits and collections and other cash-flow problems can be as hectic and stimulating as any other. The additional revenues that may be generated by "good" control in the treasurer's area of responsibility can amount to a substantial proportion of net income.

Management Accounting. The controller is involved in the third essential element of management, control. His major functions are planning operations, reporting and interpreting the results of operations, and evaluating a plan and consulting on such plans with other management. In these areas, the cost accountant provides him with important assistance. The controller also gets involved with tax administration, government reports, and protecting and safeguarding assets and the records of those assets. These functions are clearly involved with day-to-day operations.

INTERRELATIONSHIPS BETWEEN THE CONTROLLER AND OTHER EXECUTIVES

There must be an interchange of ideas and discussion of problem areas at all levels of management. For example, sales managers are deeply concerned with deliveries from the production department. By the same token, the production department has a very valid interest in the proportionate quantities of sizes, styles, and products sold, the so-called product mix. The controller is as concerned with these problems as sales and production through his function of reporting deviations from plans.

The Controller and the Treasurer. Because one of the principal functions of the controller is to evaluate and report on exceptions to the plan or budget, he has constant contact with other departments. Inasmuch as he is reporting exceptions to plans, and plans tend to be optimistic, more often than not the controller—and we here use the words controller and cost accountant synonymously—is the bearer of bad tidings. In addition to technical skills, an effective controller must achieve the savoir faire of the diplomat. In particular, the controller must avoid even the semblance of telling other department heads *how* to achieve their assigned objectives.

Obviously, there are many areas where the duties of the treasurer and controller merge. For example, the inventory figures that appear on the balance sheet and income statement as well as on the income-tax return, are of mutual concern. The functions of the cost accountant in determining inventories usually serve both financial and management accounting purposes. Fortunately, both the treasurer and the controller understand a common language, accounting, to assist them in resolving their mutual problems.

The Controller and the Production Department. The cost accountant is in daily, if not hourly, contact with the production department. It is imperative that rapport be established and maintained. Too frequently, operating departments say, "Those guys from the inky finger department are out to get me." Figures 1.2 and 1.3 indicate identical results. Labor costs are 5 percent per unit higher than planned but for entirely different reasons. Where the cost increase is due to a labor contract, production is hardly at fault for failure to meet the plan. Where labor cost exceeds the planned cost because of excessive scrap, the reason might be that less expensive materials were used and that overall costs had been reduced. In order to determine the correct cause, thorough analysis is imperative.

In several other areas there must be close cooperation and rapport. Unless source documents for cost accounting information are coordinated with the paperwork necessary to move the product through the production process, there can be a paperwork explosion with resultant inefficiency. Reporting to and by production must be swift and relevant.

The make/buy decision is an example of a problem that must be worked out jointly by production and cost accounting. Is it cheaper, considering volume of production and cost of equipment, to buy a component of our product than it is to manufacture the component ourselves? Another example of necessary joint planning concerns the question of capital budgeting. Assuming that a company can achieve lower costs by replacing some of its production facilities, is it economically feasible to do so? This could only be resolved after discussions with the treasurer, controller, and the production department (plus possibly a few other departments).

The Controller and the Sales Department. Essentially the same problems and opportunities arise between the controller and the sales department as between the controller and the production department. Insofar as control is concerned, distribution costs, including advertising and warehousing, may exceed production costs for many products. The exceptions to planned costs of distribution pose the same problems as exceptions to planned production costs.

The financial plan or budget of the firm is usually based on anticipated revenues, which in turn must come from sales of the firm's products. Therefore, it is of the utmost importance that the sales department and the controller exchange information constantly as to how sales have met the plan and how anticipated sales will meet the plan in the immediate future. Major decisions on budget revision affecting production scheduling, purchases of raw materials, and cash requirements flow from this interchange of information.

Cost accounting has developed primarily in the area of factory and production costs. Accordingly, the area of distribution cost analysis, including marketing costs, has not been fully explored. There is much room for improvement, and there will be additional discussion on this subject in chapter 16.

CHAPTER 2

The Terminology of Cost Accounting

Before one can fully understand cost accounting, its special vocabulary must be learned. One problem that cost accountants face is that some of the frequently used terms change their meaning depending on the context in which they are used.

COST

Cost is the price paid for the acquisition, maintenance, production, or use of materials or services. The meaning of the word can change, depending on the purpose for which the cost is incurred. For example, one type of cost may represent the acquisition of a fixed asset that will benefit the business for many years, such as the cost of a machine; the cost of a fixed asset that is not readily marketable and that can only be recovered by using the particular fixed asset is frequently called a *sunk cost*. Other costs represent immediate expense, such as the cost of electricity to run a machine. With no pun intended, this latter cost is called a *current cost*.

In this chapter we will be primarily concerned with the distinctions between the following kinds of costs: fixed costs and variable costs, unit costs and total costs, product costs and period costs, controllable costs and noncontrollable costs, absorption costs and direct costs, and manufacturing costs and nonmanufacturing costs.

FIXED AND VARIABLE COSTS

Accountants and managers frequently try to relate costs to sales or production in order to have meaningful bases for comparing the results of operations from one time period to another or from an operation of one size to an operation of another size. Another important use of a comparison of costs to output is to assist management in planning and controlling current operations.

Fixed Costs. Costs that do not change in relationship to output are called fixed costs. Examples of fixed costs would be the salary paid to the factory manager and the depreciation on the factory building. If we were to plot the relationship between such costs and sales on a graph, the relationship would appear as shown in Figure 2.1.

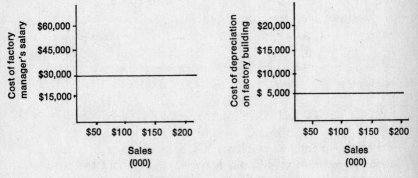

Figure 2.1. Fixed costs related to sales

It is possible to change the level of fixed costs without changing the "fixed" nature of those costs. If a company builds a new factory building, the level of fixed costs will be changed by the additional depreciation. The fixed nature of depreciation costs will not be changed. Only the level of the cost will change. The new level, of course, does not change as output changes.

Variable Costs. A variable cost changes in total with changes in activity. Examples of variable costs are sales commissions and most materials used in manufacturing as part of the direct manufacturing process. The graph of the relationship between variable costs and activity is presented in Figure 2.2 using the examples of sales commissions to sales and raw-material costs to units produced. Sales commissions are a constant 1 percent of sales, and raw-material costs are a constant $1 per unit produced.

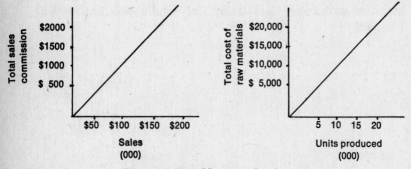

Figure 2.2. *Variable costs related to sales*

TOTAL COSTS AND UNIT COSTS

Up to this point our emphasis has been on costs in a total or absolute sense. It is difficult, however, to compare the costs of operating a factory that produces 1,000,000 units of Brand X to the costs of a factory that produces 100,000 units of Brand X. One can only say that it costs more to manufacture 1,000,000 units than it does to manufacture 100,000. The important question is whether it is more economical to operate a plant that makes 1,000,000 units than one that makes only 100,000 units. Another way of asking this question is, "Is it better to have one factory making 1,000,000 units or ten factories making 100,000 units each?" In order to provide the vocabulary used in answering the question, let us examine the difference between total costs and unit costs.

Total Costs. Total costs are the sum total of the individual costs of a project, manufacturing process, or time period without regard to the number of units produced. Thus, if all the costs incurred in manufacturing 1,000,000 units of Brand X in the larger plant were $5,000,000, this amount would be the total cost of the larger plant. Similarly, if all the costs incurred in the smaller plant were $600,000, this would be the total costs of the smaller plant.

Unit Costs. Unit costs are total costs divided by the number of appropriate units produced. The unit used will usually differ from one operating department to another, and it may be different for each department than it would be for the company as a whole. The base used to express a unit cost for one department or operation might be in terms of a physical product, while the unit used as a base in another department could be in terms of either labor hours or machine hours expended in processing the physical product. Continuing our illustration of the larger and the smaller plant, the unit costs would be as follows:

Large plant:
$$\frac{\text{Total costs}}{\text{Units produced}} \quad \frac{\$5,000,000}{1,000,000} \quad = \quad \$5 \text{ unit cost}$$

Small plant:
$$\frac{\text{Total costs}}{\text{Units produced}} \quad \frac{\$600,000}{100,000} \quad = \quad \$6 \text{ unit cost}$$

Within either plant, unit costs might be subdivided as follows:

Materials	$1 per unit
Department A costs	$.50 per unit
Department B direct-labor hours	½ hour per unit
Department C machine hours	¼ hour per unit

The importance of the definitions of cost can be illustrated by a discussion leading to a rational decision as to which size plant to build. Continuing with the example of the larger and the smaller plant, it is obvious that a $5 unit cost is preferable to a $6 unit cost. But fixed costs are fixed only with respect to total costs. Fixed costs per unit will change in an inverse ratio to changes in production. In the example of the larger plant, if $2,000,000 of the total costs of $5,000,000 are fixed costs, the fixed cost is $2 per unit as long as 1,000,000 units are produced. The reverse is true of variable costs; they tend to remain at $3 per unit no matter how many units are produced. The following illustrates the constant nature of variable costs and the changing nature of fixed costs insofar as unit costs are concerned:

Production level

1,000,000 units:

Fixed costs	$2,000,000
Variable costs (1,000,000 × $3)	3,000,000
Total costs	$5,000,000

$$\frac{\text{Costs}}{\text{Units}} = \frac{\$5,000,000}{1,000,000} = \$5 \text{ unit cost}$$

500,000 units:

Fixed costs	$2,000,000
Variable costs (500,000 × $3)	1,500,000
Total costs	$3,500,000

$$\frac{\text{Costs}}{\text{Units}} = \frac{\$3,500,000}{500,000} = \$7 \text{ unit cost}$$

1,250,000 units:

Fixed costs	$2,000,000
Variable costs (1,250,000 × $3)	3,750,000
Total costs	$5,750,000

$$\frac{\text{Costs}}{\text{Units}} = \frac{\$5,750,000}{1,250,000} = \$4.60 \text{ unit cost}$$

PRODUCT COSTS AND PERIOD COSTS

Cost accounting originally developed in the manufacturing aspects of the firm because of the ease with which internal costs could be measured and because most industrial firms were production oriented. This emphasis on production led to emphasis on the product and its use as the basis for measurement. Great pains are taken to divide costs into categories that describe their function or relation to the product. In spite of this historical relationship of cost accounting to product costs, the same concepts are adaptable to all phases of the business.

Product Costs. One of the basic methods of dividing costs into their functional categories is to describe them as either product costs or period costs. A product cost is one that "clings to" or is "attached to" a product. Normally, costs assigned to inventory can be called product costs. What is meant by this is that the product cannot be produced without incurring the cost. There are three major subcategories of product cost: raw material, direct labor, and overhead.

RAW MATERIAL. Raw material is the integral material component upon which the basic transformations occur that make it into the finished product and that can be reasonably assigned to a physical unit of output. In an oil refinery, the raw material is the unprocessed crude oil. A finished product would be the gasoline one burns in a car engine. Minor amounts of materials used in the manufacturing process may be classified as supplies or indirect material, either of which would be considered as overhead rather than raw material.

DIRECT LABOR. Direct labor is labor that is expended directly on specific products. Therefore, a production machine operator would be considered as direct labor; his wages would be a direct-labor charge. Because of the difficulty in tracing such charges to the final product in any meaningful manner, certain labor charges such as janitorial wages or the salary of the factory manager would be classified as indirect labor and would be a part of overhead.

OVERHEAD. Overhead includes all factory costs except direct labor and raw material. It is important that overhead costs be separated into two categories: fixed and variable. An example of fixed factory overhead is depreciation on the factory building and the machines used in the production process. Other examples are rent, insurance, supervisory salaries, and property taxes. Examples of variable factory overhead would include supplies, indirect labor, and power.

Period Costs. A period cost is any cost that cannot be assigned to inventory, because no value is added to the product as a consequence of incurring the cost. It is related to the current period and not to any future period. Examples of period costs are the sales manager's salary, the financial or general accountant's salary, and depreciation on a sales office building. Typically, all nonmanufacturing expenses are treated as period costs.

CONTROLLABLE AND NONCONTROLLABLE COSTS

With the growth of business enterprises it has become necessary to establish subdivisions within the company for purposes of management and control. Cost data are accumulated by area of responsibility within the organization, especially where there is some degree of decentralization of operations. The theory behind this development is that the person who is responsible for the operation of a segment of the business should be held accountable for the results of the operations. This leads to the concept of controllability of costs as a classification medium. A controllable cost is one that is reasonably subject to regulation by the division head or other executive of the segment being measured. Although any cost can be uncontrollable at a given level, all costs are controllable at some level. The higher the manager's level, the more costs are under his control. By this definition of control we are not necessarily speaking in terms of reducing the cost, but rather in terms of maintaining costs at some preplanned level. This topic will be discussed in more detail in chapter 18.

ABSORPTION AND DIRECT COSTS

In accounting for manufacturing operations, it is almost axiomatic that the costs of manufacturing a product should be included in the asset called inventory until the product is sold.

Absorption Costs. Accountants have traditionally recorded all costs of manufacturing the product as part of the cost of the product itself. This method is termed absorption costing because the full cost of the manufacturing process is "absorbed." Fixed and variable costs are handled in exactly the same manner, which means that all manufacturing costs are considered product costs and all nonmanufacturing costs are considered period costs.

Direct Costs. More and more manufacturing concerns are turning from the absorption costing technique for internal reporting to one called direct costing. By the direct costing technique only variable costs are included in the cost of the product. Fixed costs are considered period costs, even though they may be costs of production. Since both methods treat materials and direct labor as variable costs, the major area of difference lies in the application of overhead. This topic will be discussed in more detail in chapter 13.

MANUFACTURING AND NONMANUFACTURING COSTS

All costs of production are manufacturing costs. However, there are many costs of doing business that are not manufacturing costs. These include costs of selling, distribution, and administration. Accounting for these costs has not developed to the level that exists in accounting for manufacturing costs. The nonmanufacturing areas offer the greatest potential for the further development of cost accounting techniques.

CHAPTER 3

Inventory Management

For most businesses, inventories are highly significant in terms of total assets and may be the most important physical asset of a retailing or manufacturing operation. As retailing and manufacturing operations become more complex, inventory valuation and management become more difficult. Several techniques for valuing and managing inventory will be discussed in this chapter.

VALUATION OF INVENTORIES

In order to make income measurements, it is necessary to allocate costs of goods between those goods on hand at the end of the year and those sold during the year. The importance of this allocation is more apparent when one considers the income statement format of a typical company, particularly the cost-of-goods-sold section of that income statement. This section, presented below is simplified in that it ignores freight, purchase discounts, purchase returns, and so forth, and concentrates only on the basic factors.

TYPICAL CORPORATION
STATEMENT OF COST OF GOODS SOLD

Beginning inventory	$100,000
Add: Net purchases	375,000
Cost of goods available for sale	$475,000
Less: Ending inventory	90,000
Cost of goods sold	$385,000

The beginning inventory figure is obtained from the prior period statement of financial position. The ending inventory is the same number that appears on the current period statement of financial position. This method of presentation emphasizes the importance of the inventory numbers appearing on the statement of financial position but hides the significance of the inventory valuation method used to develop the numbers.

Methods of Inventory Valuation. Management must determine how it will value the inventories of the firm on its financial statements. The method of valuing inventories is important in that it directly affects the measurement of cost of goods sold and, therefore, net income. The valuation method will also determine the numbers listed for inventory on the statement of financial position.

The basic problems posed by the availability of several equally acceptable inventory techniques are in the areas of the timing of income recognition and the fluctuation of inventory acquisition costs. The name of the game is to choose the inventory valuation method that will best present management's philosophy of inventory and income measurement, minimize income taxes, minimize record-keeping costs, and provide adequate inventory control. It is an a priori condition that if there were no inventory price fluctuations there would be no difference between the results obtained by the application of the various inventory valuation techniques.

In addition to choosing between LIFO, FIFO, and average costs, the business has the option of valuing its inventory on either a periodic or a perpetual basis. *Periodic-inventory techniques* are those in which the business does not keep a running total of its inventory value or cost of goods sold. Instead, at some regular time interval, the company physically counts and prices its goods on hand. By taking the preceding count (beginning inventory), adding purchases, and subtracting the current count (ending inventory), the company deduces the cost of goods sold. Generally only two journal entries are made each year to inventory. The first journal entry would be to eliminate the beginning inventory:

Profit and loss	xxx	
Beginning inventory		xxx

The second journal entry would be to record the ending inventory:

Ending inventory	xxx	
Profit and loss		xxx

This technique has the advantage of saving most of the bookkeeping costs associated with the far more complex record-keeping requirements of a perpetual-inventory method. The drawbacks of the periodic method are the almost complete lack of book control over inventory and the paucity of profit and loss information for management between counts.

In the *perpetual-inventory method*, a running count of inventory is maintained by the business at all times. Any transaction that increases or decreases inventories will result in a debit or credit to inventory. Some appropriate journal entries for the perpetual-inventory method are listed below and are compared with the entries for a periodic method.

Journal Entries

Transaction	PERPETUAL	PERIODIC

Purchase	Inventory
	    Cash or accounts payable
		Purchases
		    Cash or accounts
		      payable

Sale	Cash or accounts receivable
	    Sales
	Cost of goods sold
	    Inventory
		Cash or accounts
		    receivable
		    Sales

Having determined the format of its inventory techniques, the firm must adopt a consistent valuation technique. There are several of these valuation techniques available; the most commonly used are FIFO, some form of average cost, and LIFO.

FIFO. FIFO is an acronym for first-in, first-out. This inventory technique treats the cost of the first inventory items acquired as a cost of goods sold. It has the advantage of stressing current costs on the statement of financial position but also the disadvantage of putting older costs on the income statement. (This is a disadvantage in times of rising prices because of the higher reported profits on which taxes are levied.) Under the FIFO method, if 600 units of raw material are purchased at $.50 per unit and, later, 400 units are purchased at a cost of $.55 per unit, the first 600 units put into production will be listed at $.50 per unit and the next 400 at $.55 per unit. Conversely, if any units remain on hand, the first 400 are priced at $.55 and the rest at $.50 per unit.

The statement of current costs on the statement of financial position is an advantage because the statement then gives a better indication of current financial position. However, carrying older costs on the income statement may be a disadvantage because the impact of inflation or deflation is included as part of operating income.

Average Costs. There are many different types of average cost techniques. Probably the two most popular methods are the weighted average and the moving average. Under the *moving-average method* the cost of each purchase is combined with the cost of the inventory on hand, and the total cost resulting from this combination is divided by the total number of units available in the inventory. Therefore, a new average unit price will be used after each purchase. This method is used with a perpetual-inventory system.

Where the *weighted-average method* is used, inventories are computed by adding the cost of the beginning inventory to the cost of purchases and dividing the total cost by the number of units available for sale. The weighted-average method is usually used with the periodic-inventory method. These average methods fall somewhere in between FIFO and LIFO in their theory of income and financial position presentation.

LIFO. LIFO is an acronym for last-in, first-out. This method puts the most current inventory costs on the income statement as cost of goods sold and shows the older costs on the statement of financial position as current inventory. The LIFO method treats the most recently received good as that which is sold first, the oldest good being considered as left in stock. Since most businesses do not operate in this manner, the LIFO method does not represent the flow of goods for them. For a better understanding of the differences between the various types of inventory valuation methods, the three techniques are illustrated in the next section.

Comparative Illustration of FIFO, Weighted-Average, and LIFO Methods. The Typical Manufacturing Corporation manufactures fine widgets out of the raw material tungsten. Its purchases and issuances of tungsten for the production process for the month of July are listed below.

TYPICAL MANUFACTURING CORPORATION
CALCULATION OF TUNGSTEN INVENTORY

	Purchases (units)	Issues (units)	Balance (units)
July 1			225 @ $1.00
July 5	160 @ $1.05		385
July 7		180	205
July 9	175 @ 1.07		380
July 15		200	180
July 21	220 @ 1.09		400
July 24		230	170
July 27	150 @ 1.10		320
July 29		120	200

Typical began the month with 225 units that cost $1 per unit. In addition, the company acquired four different sized lots of material at increasing prices. At the end of July it was found that there were 200 units on hand. This information, however, is not sufficient to enable one to determine the carrying value of the ending inventory of tungsten unless one is also told which valuation method the company is using.

Example of FIFO Inventory. If the company uses FIFO inventory measurements, it makes no difference whether it uses a periodic- or perpetual-inventory method; the final inventory value will always be the same because it will always be the value of the last goods received. In the Typical Manufacturing Corporation the ending inventory consists of 200 units (see above). Under a periodic-inventory method, the ending inventory would be composed of 150 units at $1.10 and 50 units at $1.09 (determined by calculating the last 200 units received) for a total ending inventory value of $219.50. The cost of goods transferred to production would be $765.55 using this valuation procedure. The records for a perpetual-inventory system are illustrated in Figure 3.1.

Purchases	Total	Issues	Total	Balance	Total
				July 1 225 @ $1.00	$225.00
July 5 160 @ $1.05	$168.00			July 5 160 @ 1.05 / 225 @ 1.00	393.00
		July 7 180 @ $1.00	$180.00	July 7 160 @ 1.05 / 45 @ 1.00	213.00
July 9 175 @ 1.07	187.25			July 9 175 @ 1.07 / 160 @ 1.05 / 45 @ 1.00	400.25
		July 15 155 @ 1.05 / 45 @ 1.00	207.75	July 15 175 @ 1.07 / 5 @ 1.05	192.50
July 21 220 @ 1.09	239.80			July 21 220 @ 1.09 / 175 @ 1.07 / 5 @ 1.05	432.30
		July 24 5 @ 1.05 / 175 @ 1.07 / 50 @ 1.09	247.00	July 24 170 @ 1.09	185.30
July 27 150 @ 1.10	165.00			July 27 150 @ 1.10 / 170 @ 1.09	350.30
		July 29 120 @ 1.09	130.80	July 29 150 @ 1.10 / 50 @ 1.09	219.50

Figure 3.1. Perpetual FIFO inventory method

Examples of Weighted- and Moving-Average Inventory Methods. This section will discuss the computations of the two most commonly used average inventory valuation techniques: the weighted average and the moving average.

Since the weighted-average method is generally used in conjunction with a periodic inventory rather than a perpetual-inventory technique, the company does not keep track of costs transferred out. Instead, cost of goods transferred out and cost of inventory remaining on hand are determined by calculating the total of beginning inventory costs plus purchases and dividing the total by the number of units made available. As demonstrated in Figure 3.2 this yields a weighted-average cost of

	Units	Unit cost	Total cost
July 1 (balance)	225	$1.00	$225.00
July 5	160	1.05	168.00
July 9	175	1.07	187.25
July 21	220	1.09	239.80
July 29	150	1.10	165.00
Totals	930		$985.05
Average unit cost (total cost/total units)		$1.05919	
Units remaining	200 @	$1.05919	$211.84
Units transferred out (numbers rounded)	730 @	$1.05919	$773.21

Figure 3.2. Weighted-average inventory calculation

$1.05919 per unit. Multiplying the units in ending inventory by the unit cost yields the value of ending inventory: $211.84. The balance of $773.21 is the cost of units transferred out.

Many companies that keep perpetual inventories use a moving-average inventory valuation. The use of this method is illustrated in Figure 3.3.

The inventory issued for production purposes is charged out at the average cost of the inventory on hand. The average cost of inventory on hand will change only when a new purchase is made, and then only when the new purchase is at a price different from the old average. Using the situation of the Typical Manu-

Purchases	Total	Issues	Total	Balance	Total
				July 1 225 @ $1.00	$225.00
July 5 160 @ $1.05	$168.00			5 385 @ 1.02	393.00
		July 7 180 @ $1.02	$183.60	7 205 @ 1.02	209.40
July 9 175 @ 1.07	187.25			9 380 @ 1.04	396.65
		July 15 200 @ 1.04	208.00	15 180 @ 1.04	188.65
July 21 220 @ 1.09	239.80			21 400 @ 1.07	428.45
		July 24 230 @ 1.07	246.10	24 170 @ 1.07	182.35
July 27 150 @ 1.10	165.00			27 320 @ 1.08	347.35
		July 29 120 @ 1.08	129.60	29 200 @ 1.08	217.75

Figure 3.3. Moving-average inventory method (numbers rounded)

facturing Corporation, Figure 3.3 shows an ending inventory of $217.75 and a cost of goods transferred to production of $767.30.

Illustrations of Periodic and Perpetual LIFO Methods. Within the generic category of LIFO inventory valuation techniques are two subcategories, periodic and perpetual LIFO, whose dissimilarities stem from different record-keeping methods.

Periodic LIFO is a method similar to periodic FIFO except that the earliest purchases are considered to be left in inventory and the latest transferred out. This method ignores temporary dips in quantities below the ending inventory level as long as they are made up before the balance-sheet date. In the Typical Manufacturing Corporation the ending LIFO inventory calculated on a periodic basis would be 200 units at $1, using the value per unit of the beginning inventory. Thus, closing inventory is $200 and $785.05 is charged out.

Under the perpetual LIFO system the value of the ending inventory has been affected by the temporary decline within the period to only 170 units. The value of the units transferred to production would be $782.05, while the ending inventory would be valued at $203.00, as illustrated in Figure 3.4.

PLANNING AND CONTROL OF INVENTORIES

Simultaneously with its decision as to how inventories are to be valued, the company should determine how to control inventories in order to operate at the lowest possible costs. Deciding when to buy and how much to buy can be extremely difficult. In fact, in a sophisticated model of the firm, it may be impossible to arrive at the answers to these questions without relating inventory to the corporation's entire capital structure and overall goals. Since most firms have not yet arrived at the necessary level of sophistication to enable them to find the solution to the overall problem, they must suboptimize in order to determine their best inventory levels. Our concern here will be with the optimization of inventory levels rather than the optimization of the asset values of the firm as a whole.

Offsetting Inventory Costs. Most inventory models try to offset

Purchases	Total	Issues	Total	Balance	Total
				July 1 225 @ $1.00	$225.00
July 5 160 @ $1.05	$168.00			July 5 225 @ 1.00 160 @ 1.05	393.00
		July 7 160 @ $1.05 20 @ 1.00	$188.00	July 7 205 @ 1.00	205.00
July 9 175 @ 1.07	187.25			July 9 205 @ 1.00 175 @ 1.07	392.25
		July 15 175 @ 1.07 25 @ 1.00	212.25	July 15 180 @ 1.00	180.00
July 21 220 @ 1.09	239.80			July 21 180 @ 1.00 220 @ 1.09	419.80
		July 24 220 @ 1.09 10 @ 1.00	249.80	July 24 170 @ 1.00	170.00
July 27 150 @ 1.10	165.00			July 27 170 @ 1.00 150 @ 1.00	335.00
		July 29 120 @ 1.10	132.00	July 29 170 @ 1.00 30 @ 1.10	203.00

Figure 3.4. Perpetual LIFO inventory method

the costs of acquiring and holding inventories and the opportunity costs of not having sufficient inventory on hand so that total costs are minimized. Companies hold inventories for three reasons: The first and probably the most important reason is to be able to trade goods for other goods or for money. This motive is called a *transactions motive* by many writers. If the company knows with certainty the demand for its products and if prices are not expected to change, the transactions motive would be the only reason for having inventory. In order to combat the uncertainty of business, however, companies will have on hand not only the amount they expect to sell but also an additional amount, called a *safety stock*, to guard against running out of inventory when a customer wants to buy. This second motive is called a *precautionary motive*. The third motive for acquiring inventory is a *speculative motive*. This motive comes into play when prices on inventories are expected to fluctuate. If the business expects prices to increase, it should acquire more inventory than it would if prices were to remain constant. If the company anticipates price declines, it will not buy as much inventory. Taking these motives into consideration, let us examine the costs related to inventory decisions.

Costs Related to Inventory Decisions. Generally there are three types of costs to be considered before one can establish optimal inventory policies: costs of acquiring inventories, costs of stocking inventories, and costs of running out of inventories. The costs of acquiring inventories include the costs of ordering and receiving materials, the costs of producing goods in a manufacturing concern, some of the clerical costs involved in paying for the goods or labor, inspection costs, and so on. The more common costs in carrying goods in stock are the cost of the money tied up in inventory, the cost of renting space for storage, the costs of obsolescence and deterioration of inventory, insurance costs, and taxes. The costs of not having enough inventory in stock are generally the special clerical processing costs, the special handling and shipping costs to fill back orders, and the costs of customer dissatisfaction, including the opportunity costs of lost sales. These last costs, the *stock-out costs*, are probably the most difficult costs to estimate. To come up with this number, a firm would have to determine the number of orders permanently lost because they were not processed on time; quite probably the best measure would be in gross profit on sales.

Effects of Opportunity and Joint Costs. Many of the problems related to the minimizing of total inventory costs derive from the fact that such costs are either opportunity or joint costs. Opportunity costs are not normally contained in the accounting records of a business, and their determination is frequently expensive as well as difficult. The problems relating to joint costs are more fully discussed in chapter 6.

Regardless of the difficulty in determining opportunity costs, it is absolutely necessary that such costs be given consideration in establishing corporate inventory policy. It is wise to remember in any decision process, including that concerning inventories, that the costs to be concerned with are only those costs that change. In other words, any costs that do not change from one decision to the next can be ignored. Some of these costs in inventory decisions that could be ignored would be the salaries of the controller and the accounting clerks and depreciation on the factory building. Over the years some complex and sophisticated decision models concerning inventory order quantities have evolved in order to attempt to minimize the total inventory costs. The next section of this book will examine one of the less complicated models, which should suffice to yield an insight into the significance of the three classes of inventory costs.

EOQ Formula. The most economical order size for acquisition of inventory can be determined by using a simple formula called the *economic order quantity (EOQ) formula*. In this formula

O = size of order
C = annual cost of holding one unit in inventory
Q = amount to be used
P = cost of placing and receiving an order

To find the economic order quantity, substitute the numbers determined for a given situation in the following equation:

$$O = \sqrt{\frac{2PQ}{C}}$$

This formula has been in use for at least fifty years; its derivation can be found in many cost accounting and economics textbooks. To see how this formula works, let us examine the following set of facts:

The Snygen Whiskey Cask Company reconditions used whiskey barrels. It buys used barrels from distillers at $16 per barrel. Total annual needs amount to 30,000 barrels at a rate of 100 barrels per working day. In reviewing the company's records it is found that the desired rate of return on investment is 15 percent, and the cost information below is computed.

Desired rate of return on investment in barrels, per barrel	(15% × $16)	$ 2.40
Rent, depreciation, taxes per unit per year		.50
Carrying costs per year per barrel		$ 2.90
Costs per purchase order		$14.00

CASE 1. From the EOQ formula

$$O = ?$$
$$C = \$2.90$$
$$Q = 30,000$$
$$P = \$14.00$$

Substituting into the formula and solving for O

$$O = \sqrt{\frac{2 \times 30{,}000 \times \$14.00}{\$2.90}} = \sqrt{289{,}655} = 539 \text{ bbl per order}$$
or 56 orders per year

CASE 2. If the costs per purchase order were to rise to $20

$$O = \sqrt{\frac{2 \times 30{,}000 \times \$20.00}{\$2.90}} = \sqrt{413{,}793} = 644 \text{ bbl per order}$$
or 47 orders per year

CASE 3. Using the original numbers, if carrying costs were to fall to $1.40

$$O = \sqrt{\frac{2 \times 30{,}000 \times \$14.00}{\$1.40}} = \sqrt{600{,}000} = 775 \text{ bbl per order}$$
or 39 orders per year

Thus, even if a company is not sure about the "true values" of certain opportunity costs, it can use its "best guess" costs and test the answers to see how such answers change with changes in input data. Such tests demonstrate the sensitivity of cost guesses to error. The total annual costs in Cases 1, 2, and 3 above would be:

	Case 1	Case 2	Case 3
Annual carrying costs*			
$2.90 \times \dfrac{539}{2}$	$782		
$2.90 \times \dfrac{644}{2}$		$934	
$1.40 \times \dfrac{775}{2}$			$543
Annual order costs			
14×56	784		
20×47		940	
14×39			546
Total Cost	$1,566	$1,874	$1,089

* The annual carrying costs would be equal to the average number of units in stock (beginning plus ending inventory divided by 2) or ½ the optimum order quantity times the carrying cost per unit.

(All numbers are rounded to the nearest dollar.)

To make a more significant point, assume the facts in Case 1, except that there are three companies faced with the same situation. Company 1 uses the EOQ formula approach, and Companies 2 and 3 do not. Company 2 makes more frequent orders of smaller lots, and Company 3 makes fewer orders of more barrels per order.

	Company 1	Company 2	Company 3
Number of orders	56	75	30
Number of units per order	539	400	1,000
Carrying costs			
$\dfrac{539}{2} \times 2.90$	$782		
$\dfrac{400}{2} \times 2.90$		$580	
$\dfrac{1,000}{2} \times 2.90$			$1,450
Order costs			
14×56	784		
14×75		1,050	
14×30			420
Total costs	$1,566	$1,630	$1,870

Quantity Discounts and Production Runs. Since they affect unit prices, quantity discounts will also affect the EOQ formula. The fact that quantity discounts exist makes the formula more complicated; however, no new conceptual problems are introduced.

The EOQ formula approach is also excellent for determining the size of a production run. In applying EOQ to production runs rather than to purchases, one simply substitutes the setup costs for adjusting machines or changing over from one product to another for the purchase price or the cost of purchasing.

Order Time and Safety Stocks. Of the three primary motives for carrying inventory mentioned previously, the EOQ approach is pertinent to the transaction motive. The second reason for carrying inventories, the precautionary motive, is overstocking to avoid being out of goods and thereby losing customers. If the average usage of inventory is known with certainty and the length of time between order placement and the receipt of goods is known, a company can tell exactly when merchandise should be reordered and what stocks should be kept on hand. For example, if the whiskey barrel company uses 600 barrels a week and this demand pattern does not fluctuate, and if the lead time is one week, 600 barrels would be ordered whenever the inventory level reached 600 units. Unfortunately, most businesses do not experience such a constant demand, and a problem arises when there are sudden spurts in activity or delays in delivery of inventory items. Since this is true for practically all companies, they must provide for some sort of safety stock or buffer inventory as a cushion against maximum usage. Again, in the whiskey barrel company, it might be that the company would never expect to sell more than 900 units in one week. If that were the case and the company wished never to run out of inventory, the minimum reorder point would be set at 900 units. Of this, the extra 300 units would be safety stock. This type of information can be determined at least in part by past experience. If the company were to review its records and its forecasts for the future, it could most likely come up with a probability distribution of demand for its product for usages of various quantities. The optimum safety stock would exist where the cost of carrying the extra units is exactly counterbalanced by the expected cost of not carrying those units. It should be remembered that the objective is to minimize inventory costs, not necessarily thereby to minimize inventories.

Obviously, carrying a minimum inventory or even no inventory at all cannot be the optimum solution for most businesses. This is in spite of the traditional maxim "The higher the turnover, the better the inventory manager." Traditional management has been wrong because it has not considered the opportunity costs involved in inventory management.

CHAPTER 4

Job Order Costing

By its very nature, cost accounting is a pragmatic discipline, a rational system for gathering and disseminating information. In practice, cost accounting systems range from the simplistic to the complex, from hand-posted notebook records to sophisticated electronic equipment. Empirically, the system of gathering and reporting data all too frequently becomes a fetish and a goal in itself, and the objectives of the system become secondary. Whatever system is used, it should always be remembered that its primary functions involve *control*, the reporting of significant deviations from the plan, and *planning*, the revision of existing plans or the formulation of new ones. A secondary function, at least in timing, is to provide cost-of-goods-sold and inventory figures for use in financial statements.

COST ACCOUNTING SYSTEMS

Essentially, all cost accounting systems may be described as either job order or process. Both systems may be in effect at the same time in different departments within the same plant.

Job-Order and Process Cost Systems. A *job-order system* is used where the unit of manufacture is distinguishable from other units manufactured in the same department. The unit of manufacture may in itself be a batch of similar products. For example, one job order might be used to gather the costs of assembling 1,000 three-horsepower lawn-mower motors and another job order to cover the costs of assembling 1,000 two-horsepower motors where both assembly operations were performed in the same department. As an alternative, assuming that space and time requirements made it necessary to have only 250 units of three-horsepower motors in process at one time, probably four job orders would be used. In another type of business, only one job order might be used to gather all costs involved in the erection of a building. As an alternative, the builder might subdivide the building into job orders for foundation, steel work, heating/cooling system, and so forth.

Process cost systems, which are described in chapter 5, are usually used in industries where there is nothing to distinguish one unit manufactured from another. Accordingly, they are most generally used in industries such as paper, petroleum, chemical, lumber, mining, canneries, and packing.

The essential difference between the two systems is that in a job-order system, costs are accumulated by the product (or batch of products), and in a process cost system, costs are accumulated by department. If two products (or batches) can be physically present in a department at the same time, the mere reporting of departmental costs would be meaningless in most cases. Returning to our example of lawn-mower motors, if a total of 200 units, but only 100 of each size, were worked on in a given department at the same time, dividing total departmental costs by units produced would not be meaningful because of the probable difference in the costs of materials and labor costs for different sized units.

Cost Centers. A *cost center* is any subdivision of a business where responsibility is fixed for costs incurred. A cost center need not be a department or other subdivision where goods are produced. Thus, a maintenance department is a cost center even though it does not work directly on the product. A cost center may be less than a department. In a machine shop, for example, a drilling machine, a planer, and an internal grinder may each be considered a separate cost center.

A service department should not be confused with a production department in a process cost system even though both are cost centers in which costs are controlled and applied departmentally. The difference is that no direct processing of the product takes place in the service department.

Again the emphasis is on planning and control. Assume that

the regular maintenance policy of the company is to spend $100 in preventive maintenance for every 250 hours of machine time. Both the responsibility for the maintenance and the authority to incur expense have been delegated to the appropriate manager. This is, of course, the plan. The control is dual: First, what is the quality of the preventive maintenance—how much unscheduled downtime is incurred; second, is the cost of $100 for every 250 hours exceeded?

Figures 1.2 and 1.3 (chapter 1) illustrate the basic principle of the cost center. The appropriate manager of the cost center—the department, subdepartment, or machine—has been given the responsibility to perform a particular operation on the product and the authority or means to do so. If the manager has no authority to change or control the means of production; in short, if he merely follows orders, the area under his control should not be a cost center.

Managers of cost centers frequently have the responsibility and authority both for costs applied to a product and for overhead costs. Many of the costs incurred while the product is being processed in a department can be identified with and assigned to individual units or batches. The same department will incur costs for items such as supervision, supplies, and material handling. The identifiable costs, which are called *direct costs*, and the general costs, which are called *overhead costs*, are equally subject to planning and control. In fact, where both direct and overhead costs can be incurred by the same cost center, which is the usual case, it is fruitless to plan and control one type of cost without planning and controlling the other.

The Basic Paperwork. Whether the cost system uses a duplicator to prepare forms on the cheapest brand of paper obtainable or an elaborate electronic data processing system with remote terminals, the purposes of the paperwork remain the same. The systems described in this chapter are schematic with the emphasis on cost accounting; additional information dealing with engineering and scheduling may be desirable in practice. Some companies use paperwork systems for production purposes separate from those used for cost accounting and control. There is just so much usable room on one piece of paper, and multiple copies of the same document may cause more problems than they resolve.

Even the latest electronic data processing equipment imposes some limitations on the amount of information that can follow one description. Unfortunately, a separation of forms may raise some coordinating problems as necessary deviations from plan are made during the process. For example, ⅜-inch material might have been substituted for ⁵⁄₁₆-inch material simply because of delivery promises and the unavailability of the latter. Such a substitution will result in a cost difference besides possible inventory control and reorder problems. Perhaps the best way to solve this dilemma in practice is a continued emphasis on the words "relevant information."

Job Order Sheet. A schematic job order sheet is presented in Figure 4.1. This sheet indicates that the process will involve only two departments, and it is assumed that the job order sheet itself can be used as a subsidiary ledger of work in process.

Work Ticket. Like a job order sheet, a work ticket has various formats, depending on the necessities and preferences in individual situations. The work ticket presented in Figure 4.2 indi-

---

Schematic, Inc.   Job No. _____

Customer **B & N Co.**   Routing, Dept. 10 Machine

Date promised **ASAP**   Dept. 11 Assemble

Product **2-h.p. motors**

Quantity **100**

Department 10

Material			Labor				Overhead
Date	Ref.	Amt.	Date	Ref.	Hrs.	Amt.	Base rate total

Department 11

Material			Labor				Overhead
Date	Ref.	Amt.	Date	Ref.	Hrs.	Amt.	Base rate total

Figure 4.1. Job order sheet

Time Card and Labor Distribution

Name _____

Clock No. _____

Soc. Sec. No. _____

	Monday Date		Tuesday Date		Wednesday Date		Thursday Date		Friday Date	
	IN	OUT	IN	OUT	IN	OUT	IN	OUT	IN	OUT

	Monday Date		Tuesday Date		Wednesday Date		Thursday Date		Friday Date	
	Hrs.	Amt.	Hrs.	Amt.	Hrs.	Amt.	Hrs.	Amt.	Hrs.	Amt.
Job No. Expense No.										

Figure 4.2. Work ticket

cates that the employee is hourly rated and that a timekeeper makes summary entries on the employee's clock card, the document for recording his attendance and paying his wages. A numerical coding system is usually used to describe the various things an employee works on during the day. Expense numbers are used to cover that time which is either lost or devoted to the performance of a service function, for example, machine downtime or setup time.

Stores Requisition. A simple form of stores requisition is shown in Figure 4.3. This form indicates that materials are charged directly from the storeroom to the particular job. In such a case, the stores requisition serves the dual purpose of charging the particular job and relieving raw materials inventory. It is a frequent practice to relieve raw materials inventory and charge the department for stores that are transferred in bulk. A subsidiary set of books kept within the department is then used to charge the particular job. Obviously, the final result is identical with that described here.

Stores Requisition				
Received by _____		Stock Code _____		
Date	Job/Expense No.*	Quantity	Unit Price	Total

*Expense numbers are used to cover the consumption of materials that do not become finished goods, for example, stock used in setting up a job. Scrap will be discussed in chapter 16.

Figure 4.3. Stores requisition

GENERAL LEDGER

The work of the cost accountant is not generally associated with general ledger entries. Ordinarily, entries in the general ledger are too formal for the necessary work of the cost accountant. By the same token, the necessary detail of the cost accountant is usually too voluminous for the general ledger.

Materials. When materials are purchased, the entry will ordinarily be:

> Inventory—Raw materials
> Accounts payable

Like all entries shown here, the above may well be part of an elaborate voucher system. Further, in a firm of any size, there will normally be a numerical coding of the raw materials for stores-control purposes.

Upon requisition for a particular job, the entry would be:

> Inventory—Work in process—Materials—Job number
> Inventory—Raw materials

If the department is charged, the entry would be:

> Inventory—Raw materials in process—Department
> Inventory—Raw materials

Then, when the materials are actually used on a job, the entry would be:

Inventory—Work in process—Materials—Job number
Inventory—Raw materials in process—Department

Upon completion of fabrication, the materials become part of the inventory of finished goods:

Inventory—Finished goods
Inventory—Work in process—Materials

One major reason for using separate general ledger accounts for the several classes of inventories is to facilitate control of the production process by management. Another reason is to provide more information on the liquidity of these inventories for creditors and others. Normally, the closer to completion the inventory comes, the more liquid that inventory is.

Labor. The source from which labor costs are determined in manufacturing is the payroll register of hourly rated employees. There is nothing inconsistent, however, in incurring direct-labor charges from payments made to salaried employees. The entries are summarized in the same format as the charges for materials:

Work in process—Labor—Job number
Accrued payroll and withholdings

or

Work in process—Labor—Job number
Work in process—Department

then

Inventory—Finished goods
Work in process—Labor—Job number

Overhead. The charging of overhead as one of the costs in manufacturing is, mechanically, extremely simple. On the other hand, the theory of how much overhead to charge is the most difficult and complex in the entire field of cost accounting. The subject is treated in detail in chapter 8; accordingly, the discussion here will be confined to the entries. The general ledger treatment of overhead is as follows:

Factory overhead control
Accounts payable

or

Accrued expenses
  (e.g., Vacation pay)

or

Allowance accounts
  (e.g., Allowance for depreciation)

or

Asset accounts
  (e.g., Prepaid insurance)

After the completion of the job order or at the end of the accounting period, the treatment is as follows:

Work in process—Overhead—Job number
  Factory overhead control

or

Work in process—Overhead—Department
  Factory overhead control

then

Work in process—Overhead—Job number
  Work in process—Overhead—Department

finally

Inventory—Finished goods
  Work in process—Overhead—Job number

The rate at which overhead is charged and the basis on which it is charged will be covered thoroughly in chapter 8. Most frequently, overhead is charged as a percentage of direct-labor dollars or as a fixed dollar amount on direct-labor hours. The basis of charging overhead may well be different between departments in the same plant.

SUBSIDIARY LEDGERS

There are simply too many entries involving cost accounts for them to be given general ledger treatment either individually or by the job. Control accounts in the general ledger are normally used for single monthly debit and credit entries, and the detail is kept in subsidiary ledgers. The word ledger, of course, embraces many types of loose-leaf and electronic records.

Work-in-process Ledger. Whether costs are charged directly to a job or to a department, it eventually becomes necessary to charge each job with all the costs incurred. This means that each job record will show an accumulation of costs incurred to date for labor and materials and overhead. The usual practice is to keep separate records for labor and for materials while a job is in a particular department, and then to enter a total including overhead on a comprehensive summary when the job is transferred to another department or to inventory—finished goods. The job sheet illustrated in Figure 4.1 could be used as a subsidiary record. The direct analogy is to accounts receivable where literally millions of individual transactions are posted to thousands of individual accounts. The theory is not difficult; the system used must be adapted to individual needs in terms of the number of transactions.

Schematic Illustration of Job Costing. A series of T-accounts will be used to summarize the material just discussed. T-accounts are illustrative ledger pages showing only the dollar amounts of debit and credit entries, together with an identifying reference. Thus, the first transaction in Figure 4.4 is a debit of $10,000 to Raw Materials and a credit to Accounts Payable, both identified as *1*.

Our exemplary company is a new firm which manufactures two- and three-horsepower electronic motors in two departments, 10 and 11. Department 10 machines stock; Department 11 assembles the machined part from Department 10 with two purchased pieces, designated Parts 609 and 709. Mr. Able supervises Department 10; Mr. Baker, Department 11. Able is paid $1,000 monthly; Baker, $900. Both report to the president. To simplify our illustration, all other factory overhead (rent, heat, light, power, depreciation) is divided 60 percent, Department 10; 40 percent, Department 11.

Our series of events assumes a journal entry is made for each transaction. In actual practice, only summary entries would be

Work in Process—Overhead

Debit	Credit
3,800 11.	15. 8,500

Accounts Payable

Debit	Credit
	10,000 1.
	1,600 2.
	2,500 3.

Accrued Overhead Expenses

Debit	Credit
	6,000 14.

Work in Process—Materials

Debit	Credit
7. 1,000	1,700 11.
8. 700	
9. 1,500	
12. 700	
13. 1,250	

Overhead Control

Debit	Credit
4. 200	8,500 15.
5. 100	
5. 100	
5. 100	
6. 1,900	
7. 100	
14. 6,000	

Payroll Withholdings

Debit	Credit
	150 4.
	300 5.
	300 5.
	300 5.
	285 6.

Work in Process—Labor

Debit	Credit
4. 800	3,200 11.
5. 1,900	
5. 1,900	
5. 1,900	

Inventory—Raw Materials

Debit	Credit
1. 10,000	1,100 7.
2. 1,600	700 8.
3. 2,500	1,500 9.
	700 12.
	1,250 13.

Finished Goods

Debit	Credit
11. 8,700	

Accrued Payroll

Debit	Credit
	850 4.
	1,700 5.
	1,700 5.
	1,700 5.
	1,615 6.

Figure 4.4. General ledger accounts

Department 10 Overhead Control

| 15. 5,200 | 1,800 | 10. |
| | 3,450 | 16. |

Department 11 Overhead Control

| 15. 3,300 | 2,000 | 10. |
| | 1,000 | 16. |

Job 101

Department 10 Labor
| 4. 800 |
| 5. 400 |

Department 11 Labor
| 5. 1,000 |
| 5. 1,000 |

Department 10 Overhead
| 10. 1,800 |

Department 11 Overhead
| 10. 2,000 |

Materials
| 7. 1,000 |
| 8. 700 |

Job 102

Department 10 Labor
| 5. 500 |
| 5. 900 |
| 5. 100 |

Department 11 Labor
| 5. 1,000 |

Department 10 Overhead
| 16. 2,250 |

Department 11 Overhead
| 16. 1,000 |

Materials
| 9. 1,500 |
| 12. 700 |

Job 103

Department 10 Labor
| 5. 800 |

Department 11 Labor
| |

Department 10 Overhead
| 16. 1,200 |

Department 11 Overhead
| |

Materials
| 13. 1,250 |

Figure 4.5. Subsidiary ledger accounts

made in the general ledger or subsidiary ledgers. Chronological sequence is not important in the illustration.

1. Bar stock is purchased and delivered to the plant. $10 of this material is used to manufacture the two-horsepower unit; $15, to manufacture the three-horsepower unit.

   Entry: General ledger (Figure 4.4)

2. Eight hundred units of Part 609 (cost $2 each) are purchased and delivered to the plant. (One part is used with each two- or three-horsepower unit.)

   Entry: General ledger

3. Five hundred units of Part 709 (cost $5 each) are purchased and delivered to the plant. (One part is used with each two- or three-horsepower unit.)

   Entry: General ledger

4. The first weekly payroll is paid. Withholdings are assumed to be 15 percent of gross payroll. Only Department 10 works this week. The work tickets show $200 was spent on setup time and $800 on direct labor—Job Order 101.

   Entry: General ledger
   Subsidiary ledger (Figure 4.5)

5. The payrolls are paid for the remainder of the month. Setup time in Department 10 is $100 each week.

   Entry: General ledger
   Subsidiary ledger

6. Salaries are paid.

   Entry: General ledger

7. Raw materials for Job Order 101 are requisitioned into Department 10. Job Order 101 calls for 100 two-horsepower motors. $100 of materials are consumed in setting up the first job.

   Entry: General ledger
   Subsidiary ledger

8. Job Order 101 is completed in Department 10 and sent to Department 11. Department 11 requisitions 100 each of Parts 609 and 709.

   Entry: General ledger
   Subsidiary ledger

9. Raw materials for Job Order 102 are requisitioned into Department 10. Job Order 102 calls for 100 three-horsepower motors.

   Entry: General ledger
   Subsidiary ledger

10. The labor on Job Order 101 is completed. It has been estimated that overhead will be 150 percent of direct-labor costs in Depart-

ment 10 and 100 percent of direct-labor costs in Department 11.
   Entry: Subsidiary ledger

11. The finished product from Job Order 101 is sent to finished goods.
    Entry: General ledger

12. Job Order 102 is sent to Department 11, and materials are requisitioned.
    Entry: General ledger
    Subsidiary ledger

13. Raw materials for Job Order 103 are requisitioned into Department 10. Job Order 103 calls for 125 two-horsepower motors.
    Entry: General ledger
    Subsidiary ledger

14. Entry is made for all other overhead incurred during the month.
    Entry: General ledger

15. Overhead is distributed to the appropriate departments.
    Entry: General ledger
    Subsidiary ledger

16. Absorbed overhead is posted to the jobs in process.
    Entry: Subsidiary ledger

The detail of overhead distribution is as follows:

Department 10		*Department 11*	
Setup time	200	Salaries	900
	100	40% of 6,000	2,400
	100		3,300
	100		
Materials	100		
Salary	1,000		
60% of 6,000	3,600		
	5,200		

A trial balance of the general ledger shows the following balance:

Inventory—Raw materials	8,850	
Work in process—Labor	3,300	
Work in process—Materials	3,450	
Work in process—Overhead	4,700	
Finished goods	8,700	
Accounts payable		14,100
Accrued payroll		7,565
Payroll withholdings		1,335
Accrued overhead expenses		6,000
	29,000	29,000

The subsidiary ledgers agree with their controls as shown in the general ledger:

Overhead Control Trial Balance

Dept. 10—Overhead control	(50)
Dept. 11—Overhead control	300
Job Order 102—Overhead	3,250
Job Order 103—Overhead	1,200
Work in process—Overhead	4,700

Labor Control Trial Balance

Job Order 102—Labor—Dept. 10	1,500
Job Order 102—Labor—Dept. 11	1,000
Job Order 103—Labor—Dept. 10	800
Work in process—Labor	3,300

Materials Control Trial Balance

Job Order 102—Materials	2,200
Job Order 103—Materials	1,250
Work in process—Materials	3,450

FINANCIAL STATEMENTS

The general ledger control accounts, substantiated by the detailed subsidiary ledgers, are the basis for several line items appearing on the financial statements of the company. Ideally, as in our simple example, there is no problem; the subsidiary accounts balance with their controls.

Empirically, however, the reconciliation is by no means so simple. The primary purpose of cost accounting, to provide data for planning and controlling, is not necessarily commensurate with the publishing of financial statements by a given date. Permitting differences to exist between control figures and the subsidiary data for interim statement purposes is a possible solution; however, this solution in turn raises potential problems in reconciling differences in reports covering the same transactions.

Work in Process. The work-in-process figure from our hypothetical general ledger (Figure 4.4) that would usually be presented in financial statements is $11,450, which we arrive at as follows:

Labor—Job Order 102—Dept. 10	$1,500	
Labor—Job Order 103—Dept. 10	800	$ 2,300
Labor—Job Order 102—Dept. 11		1,000
Materials—Job Order 102—Dept. 10	$1,500	
Materials—Job Order 102—Dept. 11	700	$ 2,200
Materials—Job Order 103—Dept. 10		1,250
Overhead—Job Order 102—Dept. 10	$2,250	
Overhead—Job Order 102—Dept. 11	1,000	$ 3,250
Overhead—Job Order 103—Dept. 10		1,200
Underabsorbed overhead—Dept. 11	$ 300	
Less: Overabsorbed overhead—Dept. 10	50	250
Work in process		$11,450

Over- or Underabsorbed Overhead. When the predetermined overhead rate is not exactly the same as the actual rate in a given accounting period, as is usually the case, there are three possible ways to deal with the problem. One method is to treat the net over- or underabsorbed figure as an addition to, or reduction of, inventories as illustrated in the example above.

Another method of dealing with the problem is to charge or credit over- or underabsorbed overhead to cost of goods sold. That is, inventories of work in process are carried at the predetermined rates, and the over- or underabsorbed balance is treated as an expense or income for the accounting period. Had this method been adopted in the example above, the inventory of work in process would have been $11,200.

A third treatment is purported to be more correct theoretically, particularly for year-end statements. It calls for applying the actual rate of overhead to all the production of the accounting period, not just to that part of the production remaining in work in process. The following is a computation for the schematic series of transactions given in this chapter:

$$\text{Dept. 10} \quad \frac{\text{Actual overhead}}{\text{Actual direct labor}} \quad \frac{(5,200)}{(3,500)} = 148.6\%$$

$$\text{Dept. 11} \quad \frac{\text{Actual overhead}}{\text{Actual direct labor}} \quad \frac{(3,300)}{(3,000)} = 110\%$$

Applying these rates to the three work orders:

	Dept. 10	Dept. 11
Work Order 101	1,783	2,200
Work Order 102	2,229	1,100
Work Order 103	1,188	
	5,200	3,300

(Figures rounded)

Therefore, finished goods inventory (Job Order 101) would be valued as follows:

Labor—Dept. 10	$1,200
Overhead—Dept. 10	1,783
Labor—Dept. 11	2,000
Overhead—Dept. 11	2,200
Materials—Dept. 10	1,000
Materials—Dept. 11	700
	$8,883

Work in process would then be as follows:

Labor—Job Order 102—Dept. 10	$1,500	
Labor—Job Order 103—Dept. 10	800	$ 2,300
Labor—Job Order 102—Dept. 11		1,000
Materials—Job Order 102—Dept. 10	$1,500	
Materials—Job Order 102—Dept. 11	700	$ 2,200
Materials—Job Order 103—Dept. 10		1,250
Overhead—Job Order 102—Dept. 10	$2,229	
Overhead—Job Order 102—Dept. 11	1,100	$ 3,329
Overhead—Job Order 103—Dept. 10		1,188
Work in process		$11,267

Whatever one concludes about the theoretical propriety of this third treatment, its practical application could be staggering. Where production from many different work orders remains in finished goods inventory and literally thousands of job orders have been processed during the accounting period, the method hardly appears to have practical merit.

CHAPTER 5

Process Cost Accounting

Process cost accounting is the system under which manufacturing costs are accumulated in total and then allocated to units on an average basis. Process costing is usually applied in a manufacturing situation where production is continuous in nature rather than in a situation calling for job cost accounting, covered in chapter 4, in which the units of production can readily be identified individually or in small batches.

EQUIVALENT UNITS OF PRODUCTION

Process costs are in reality average costs. These average costs are obtained by accumulating material, labor, and overhead costs and recording them by department or by process. If the firm produces only one product, the development of a process cost system is relatively easy. First, determine total manufacturing cost and divide the total cost by the total units produced. This yields the per unit cost. Second, multiply the number of units sold by the per unit cost to compute the total cost of goods sold. Third, multiply the number of units in the ending inventory by the unit cost to obtain the value of the ending inventory. As long as there is no work in process or at least no change in work in process at the beginning or at the end of the accounting period, this procedure is sufficient. However, when there are changing work-in-process inventories or abnormal spoilage or waste problems, it will be necessary to employ a concept known as equivalent units of production to determine process costing.

The following example illustrates the computation of equivalent units:

Beginning inventory, in process	0
Units placed in process	25,000
Units finished	22,000
Units in process at end of period ¼ finished	3,000
Total costs	$45,500

If the flow of all costs is constant throughout the production process, an average unit cost can be derived. In computing an average unit cost it is obvious that any incomplete units in the calculation should be counted only for the proportion finished during the period. Since the partially completed units have received only about one-fourth of all of the work that the finished units have received, we should give them only their equivalent weight in our computations. This means that the units in process at the end of the period will receive only one quarter of the weight that the finished units would receive on a per unit basis. To apply this to the example above, equivalent units would be calculated as follows: First, determine the units completed and transferred out of the department, either into finished goods or into another department; second, determine the number of units completed but remaining in the department; finally, determine the number of units that are still in process for which the state of completion must be estimated. Figure 5.1 illustrates this procedure.

Units finished	22,000
Ending units in process × percentage of completion (3,000 × 25%)	750
Total equivalent units completed	22,750
Total costs	$45,500
Unit cost of equivalent unit $\dfrac{\$45,500}{22,750}$	$2.00
Costs attached to finished units 22,000 × $2.00	$44,000
Costs attached to work in process 750 × $2.00	1,500
Total costs accounted for	$45,500

Figure 5.1. Computation of cost of equivalent units

Determining the Degree of Completion of Work in Process. It is quite difficult to develop any one method for determining the stage of completion of work in process. In some firms it is possible to compute the degree of completion with a high degree of accuracy simply by calculating the total process time against the time the current production has been in process. Where many departments are involved, it is sometimes assumed that all work in process at the end of a given period is one-half completed rather than computing the stages of completion for each department. As a further simplification in computation, where manufacturing overhead is applied on the basis of labor hours or hours in process, the same ratio of completion is used for overhead costs as for the total process. While this assumption serves to simplify the calculation, accuracy is hardly increased.

Inaccuracies, however, may not be too meaningful as a practical matter. Assume 20 one-day processes per month. Further assume that beginning and closing inventories are arbitrarily stated as one-half completed. If opening inventories were actually three-fourths completed and ending inventories one-fourth completed, the total error in computing average unit costs would be about 5 percent.

Interdepartmental Transfers Using the Weighted-Average Method. Up to this point, the focus has been on the treatment of equivalent units of production for a one-department factory or for one department in a factory. The next point of concern is the treatment and the cost equivalent units of production in transfers between departments in a multidepartment factory. The simplest treatment is shown in Figures 5.2 and 5.3. These figures are a production cost report for a company with two departments showing a transfer of physical goods and the transfer of the costs after determination of the equivalent units of production.

Initiating Department: Explanation of Figure 5.2. Figure 5.2 illustrates only Department A in which the processing begins. It is assumed that all the materials used in the process are inserted at the very beginning and that labor and overhead are applied in an even flow throughout. Beginning inventories in Department A are 100 percent completed as to materials and two-thirds completed as to labor and overhead. Thirty thousand new units are started into process during the accounting period, and 6,000 partially completed units are on hand at the end of the period. Lines 1 to 6, Figure 5.2, outline the foregoing in terms of units only. Although line 6 shows that 41,000 equivalent units have been worked on, actually only 31,000 were worked on during the accounting period:

⅓ of total work on 15,000 units	5,000
All work on 24,000 units	24,000
⅓ of total work on 6,000 units	2,000
	31,000

However, the costs from the previous accounting period that are connected with the 15,000 partially completed units in beginning inventory are also included in the determination of costs starting at line 8 of Figure 5.2. Thus, the average cost derived in Figure 5.2 includes some costs incurred in the previous accounting period, as well as all current period costs. It is necessary to separate the dollars as well as the equivalent unit completions between materials on the one hand and labor and overhead on the other, because all the material was inserted at the beginning of the process; whereas overhead and labor are not completed on the 6,000 units still in inventory at the end of the period.

Department Receiving the Transfer: Explanation of Figure 5.3. Department B, as depicted in Figure 5.3, receives the product from Department A. As in Department A, materials are added at the beginning of the process while labor and overhead are added uniformly throughout. The actual units processed during the month are 47,500.

⅔ of total work on 18,000 units	12,000
All work on 32,000 units	32,000
½ of total work on 7,000 units	3,500
	47,500

Again, the opening inventory costs are averaged in with costs incurred during the current month.

Interdepartmental Transfers Using FIFO. There is an alternative to the use of the weighted-average method illustrated in Figures 5.2 and 5.3. Many cost accountants argue that FIFO

SKIDER CORPORATION
PRODUCTION COST REPORT
MONTH ENDED JULY 31, 1972

Weighted-Average Cost

Department A

Equivalent Units

Determination of Units	*Unit Flow of Goods*	*Materials*	*Labor and Overhead*	*Cost per Equivalent Unit*
1. Beginning work in process	15,000 (⅔)*			
2. Units started	30,000			
3. Units to account for	45,000			
4. Units completed	39,000	39,000	39,000	
5. Ending work in process	6,000 (⅓)*	6,000	2,000	
6. Units accounted for	45,000	45,000	41,000	

Determination of Costs	*Cost Totals*	*Materials*	*Labor and Overhead*	
7. Beginning work in process	$ 9,000	$ 6,000	$ 3,000	
8. Current period costs	56,500	39,000	17,500	
9. Total costs to account for	$65,500	$45,000	$20,500	
10. Equivalent units		÷45,000	÷41,000	

		$1.00	$0.50	$1.50
11. Cost per equivalent unit				

Summary of Costs

12. Units completed (39,000)	$58,500			(39,000) ($1.50)
13. Ending work in process:				
14. Costs transferred in	—			
15. Materials	$ 6,000	(6,000) ($1.00)		
16. Labor and overhead	1,000		(2,000) ($0.50)	
17. Total cost of work in process	7,000			
18. Total costs accounted for	$65,500			

* Two-thirds of the labor needed to complete the beginning inventory of work in process was expended in the prior accounting period. All the materials were added in the prior accounting period. The inventory on hand at the end of the accounting period is complete insofar as materials are concerned. It is one-third complete as to labor.

Figure 5.2. Weighted-average cost method, Department A

SKIDER CORPORATION
Production Cost Report
Month Ended July 31, 1972

Department B

Weighted-Average Cost

Determination of Units	Unit Flow of Goods	Units Transferred In	Materials	Labor and Overhead	Cost per Equivalent Unit
			Equivalent units		
1. Beginning work in process	18,000 (⅓) *				
2. Units transferred in	39,000				
3. Units to account for	57,000				
4. Units completed	50,000	50,000	50,000	50,000	
5. Ending work in process	7,000 (½) *	7,000	7,000	3,500	
6. Units accounted for	57,000	57,000	57,000	53,500	

Determination of Costs	Cost Totals	Costs Transferred In	Materials	Labor and Overhead	Cost per Equivalent Unit
7. Beginning work in process	$ 53,400	$26,100	$21,950	$ 5,350	
8. Current period costs	150,950	58,500	55,000	37,450	

9. Total costs to account for	$204,350	$84,600	$76,950	$42,800
10. Equivalent units		÷57,000	÷57,000	÷53,500
11. Cost per equivalent unit		$1.484211	$1.35	$0.80	$3.634211

Summary of Costs

12. Units completed (50,000)	$181,711	(50,000)($3.634211)
13. Ending work in process:		
14. Costs transferred in	$ 10,389	(7,000)($1.484211)
15. Materials	9,450	(7,000)($1.35)
16. Labor and overhead	2,800	(3,500)($0.80)
17. Total cost of work in process	$ 22,639	
18. Total costs accounted for	$204,350	

Figure 5.3. Weighted-average cost method, Department B

* Degree of completion for labor and overhead. Materials 100% completed.

55

(first-in, first-out) is a more meaningful method. There are two cogent reasons for preferring FIFO. First, the inventory physically present at the end of one accounting period will be the first to be processed and transferred out in the subsequent accounting period. Second, for control purposes it is preferable that each accounting period be treated separately.

Whatever its theoretical merits, there are relatively few situations where FIFO can be used without some modification. If the production represented by the opening inventory can be kept physically separated throughout the manufacturing process, "pure" FIFO could be used. This is tantamount to a job-lot costing application in a process industry. Such a system would not be practicable where there are many producing departments, each with substantial opening and closing inventories. Moreover, there is a question whether or not the large increase in clerical expense that might be necessary is, in fact, worth the results obtained. Other difficult problems are raised when, after production is completed in the original department, units are added or lost in subsequent processing.

Figure 5.4 illustrates a modified FIFO method. It is called modified because the costs incurred during the accounting period are averaged in order to determine unit costs. No attempt is made to ascertain costs for each processing run.

Initiating Department: Explanation of Figure 5.4. Figure 5.4 should be compared with Figure 5.2 for an illustration of the difference in treatment between the weighted-average method and the modified FIFO method. Note that the equivalent units of materials are 30,000 in Figure 5.4 and 45,000 in Figure 5.2. Similarly, equivalent units of labor and overhead are 31,000 and 41,000 respectively. In the computation of unit costs, only costs incurred in this accounting period are used because only equivalent units from the accounting period are considered. Insofar as the beginning inventory is concerned, only those costs actually incurred in this period are added to the opening dollar inventories and are deemed to be the first materials transferred out. Thus, 5,000 equivalent units of labor and overhead at the current month's cost of $.564516 are added and transferred out ($2,823, line 20 of Figure 5.4). Insofar as the remaining computations are concerned, they are in principle exactly the same as those in Figure 5.2, although the dollar amounts necessarily differ.

Department Receiving the Transfer: Explanation of Figure 5.5. Figure 5.5 treats Department B under the modified FIFO cost method and should be compared with Figure 5.3. The costs transferred into Department B in Figure 5.5 differ from those transferred in Figure 5.3 because of the differences in costs transferred out between Figures 5.2 and 5.3.

LOST OR ADDED UNITS. In practice, another modification of the "pure" FIFO method is frequently used where units of production may be lost or spoiled in a department other than the one that initiates the processing. Beginning inventories are separated into costs transferred into the department and costs incurred in the department. The transferred-in costs in beginning inventory are then averaged with costs transferred in during the current month. Thus:

	DEPARTMENT B	
Units from Department A in beginning inventory	1,000	$ 3,599
Units transferred in from Department A	5,000	10,797
		$14,396
Units transferred out or in closing inventory	5,900	
Cost per unit for Department A processing		$ 2.44

Another modification of the "pure" FIFO method is necessary where units are added in subsequent processing. This treatment is the opposite of that for lost units.

	DEPARTMENT B	
Units from Department A in beginning inventory	1,000	$ 3,599
Units transferred in from Department A	5,000	10,797
		$14,396
Units transferred out or in closing inventory	6,100	
Cost per unit for Department A processing		$ 2.36

The lost or added units could result from evaporation or, as in a chemical process, from the addition of gallonage in Department B.

Modified FIFO Cost

SKIDER CORPORATION
Production Cost Report
Month Ended July 31, 1972

Department A

| | | *Equivalent Units* | |
Determination of Units	*Unit Flow of Goods*	*Materials*	*Labor and Overhead*
1. Beginning work in process	15,000 (⅔)*		
2. Units started	30,000		
3. Units to account for	45,000		
4. Units completed:			
5. From beginning inventory	15,000		5,000
6. From current production	24,000	24,000	24,000
7. Ending work in process	6,000 (⅓)*	6,000	2,000
8. Units accounted for	45,000	30,000	31,000

Determination of Costs	*Cost Totals*	*Materials*	*Labor and Overhead Cost per Equivalent Unit*
9. Beginning work in process	$ 9,000		
10. Current period costs	56,500	$39,000	$17,500
11. Total costs to account for	$65,500		
12. Equivalent units		÷30,000	÷31,000
13. Cost per equivalent unit		$ 1.300000	$ 0.564516
			$1.864516

58

Summary of Costs

14. Units completed (39,000)
15. From beginning inventory (15,000) . . . . $ 9,000
16. Current costs added:
17.   Materials   —   (5,000) ($0.564516)
18.   Labor and overhead   2,823
19. Total from beginning inventory $11,823
20. Started and completed (24,000)   44,748   (24,000) ($1.864516)
21. Total costs transferred out $56,571
22. Ending work in process (6,000):
23.   Materials $ 7,800   (6,000) ($1.300000)
24.   Labor and overhead   1,129   (2,000) ($0.564516)
25. Total cost of work in process $ 8,929
26. Total costs accounted for $65,500

* Degree of completion for labor and overhead. Materials 100% completed.

Figure 5.4. Modified FIFO cost method, Department A

59

SKIDER CORPORATION
Production Cost Report
Month Ended July 31, 1972

Department B

Modified FIFO Cost

			Equivalent Units	
Determination of Units	Unit Flow of Goods	Units Transferred In	Materials	Labor and Overhead
1. Beginning work in process	18,000 (⅓)*			
2. Units transferred in	39,000			
3. Units to account for	57,000			
4. Units completed:				
5. From beginning inventory	18,000			12,000
6. From current production	32,000	32,000	32,000	32,000
7. Ending work in process	7,000 (½)*	7,000	7,000	3,500
8. Units accounted for	57,000	39,000	39,000	47,500

				Cost per
Determination of Costs	Cost Totals	Costs Transferred In	Materials	Labor and Overhead	Equivalent Unit
9. Beginning work in process	$ 53,400			
10. Current period costs	149,021	$56,571	$55,000	$37,450
11. Total costs to account for	$202,421			
12. Equivalent units		÷39,000	÷39,000	÷47,500
13. Cost per equivalent unit		$ 1.450538	$ 1.410256	$ 0.788421	$3.649215

60

Summary of Costs

14.	Units completed (50,000)			
15.	From beginning inventory (18,000)	$ 53,400		
16.	Current costs added:			
17.	Materials	—		
18.	Labor and overhead	9,461	(12,000)	($0.788421)
19.	Total from beginning inventory	$ 62,861		
20.	Started and completed (32,000)	116,775	(32,000)	($3.649215)
21.	Total costs to finished goods	$179,636		
22.	Ending work in process (7,000):			
23.	Costs transferred in	$ 10,154	(7,000)	($1.450538)
24.	Materials	9,872	(7,000)	($1.410256)
25.	Labor and overhead	2,759	(3,500)	($0.788421)
26.	Total cost of work in process	$ 22,785		
27.	Total costs accounted for	$202,421		

* Degree of completion for labor and overhead. Materials 100% completed.

Figure 5.5. Modified FIFO cost method, Department B

JOURNAL ENTRIES UNDER WEIGHTED-AVERAGE AND FIFO PROCESS METHODS

The journal entries to record acquisition of raw materials and the application of labor and overhead to the production process are the same regardless of whether weighted-average or FIFO cost methods are used. The differences in journal entries do not appear until recording the interdepartmental transfers. The journal entry for materials would be:

Work in process—Department A	39,000	
Work in process—Department B	55,000	
Stores Control		94,000

The journal entry for labor and overhead would be:

Work in process—Department A	17,500	
Work in process—Department B	37,450	
Payroll and/or various overhead accounts		54,950

With one exception there is no difference between these journal entries and the journal entries that would be necessary under a job-order system. The exception is that in a job-order system, work in process for Jobs 1 and 2 would be debited instead of work in process for Department A and Department B. The journal entry to record the cost transferred from Department A to Department B would appear as follows under the weighted-average cost system:

Work in process—Department B	58,500	
Work in process—Department A		58,500

Using the modified FIFO cost system, the journal entry would be:

Work in process—Department B	56,571	
Work in process—Department A		56,571

Spoilage and lost units present no additional conceptual problems; however, how to handle them can be an enormously complex task. The problems of scrap, spoiled production, and waste are discussed in chapter 7.

CHAPTER 6

Joint-product and By-product Costs

Large and important segments of industry find themselves in the difficult position of being unable to determine a true product cost for many of their products. The difficulty arises when several products are made from the same basic raw materials and two or more finished products emerge simultaneously from the same inputs; these are so-called joint products. Some industries plagued by the problem are petroleum, packing, mining, and lumber. The difficulty is illustrated by the saying, "One does not slaughter a hog merely to manufacture a pair of pigskin gloves."

The fact that there is no absolute method of determining the cost of individual joint products does not mean that the cost accountant loses his traditional roles in planning and controlling. Obviously, it is impossible to control the cost of the pigskin as a separate product from pork bellies. However, it is relatively easy to set up departmental or functional budgets and then to control the costs of the departments and functions. That is, the costs of the department that removes the hides from the carcasses can be budgeted, and the department can then be controlled both as to expenditures and as to units processed against those expenditures.

TERMINOLOGY

In many areas of accounting, terms have specific meanings in one branch of the subject but mean something different when used elsewhere. Accordingly, the following section will define as precisely as possible the various terms used in this chapter for this particular branch of cost accounting.

Joint-product Costs. In this chapter, joint-product costs are those costs incurred in processing before the separate products emerge. In the example of the hog, the cost of skinning the carcass is a joint-product cost of all products coming from the hog—pigskin gloves, pork chops, bacon, and so on. It might be true that the main purpose of skinning the hog was to get the hide; nonetheless, it is not possible to obtain the rest without first removing the hide. It has been said that the entire hog is used except for the squeal. However, not all of the parts of the hog are necessarily defined as joint products. The term is usually reserved for those products which have a significant sales value compared with the total.

By-product Costs. One of the qualifications of a joint product is that it have a significant sales value compared with the total. Any other products of joint processing are usually called by-products. Unfortunately (or fortunately, if that be your point of view), there are no hard-and-fast rules to follow. Furthermore, technological change may very well alter the designation of a part as either joint product or by-product. For example, kerosene was once the principal salable product derived from the refining of petroleum. Now gasoline and heating oil are equally or more important. In recent years, in fact, a new, highly profitable line of fertilizers has become an important by-product of petroleum refining. A few years ago such by-products were being thrown away as wastes.

Scrap. Technically, any residue from production that is not the result of a mistake is a joint product. It can be argued that the turnings generated by machining on a lathe are a joint product because they emerge together with the machined part from the manufacturing process. However, the turnings fail the test of having significant sales value compared with the total. Since scrap does have some value, the distinction between it and by-product is by no means as clear. The accounting treatment of by-product and scrap may be identical. Probably the main distinction is that scrap is usually sold or recycled as a raw material, whereas a by-product is sold as a finished or semifinished product.

Waste. Residue of a process that has no salable value is waste. Frequently it has negative value in the sense that additional costs may be incurred in disposal. It is quite possible that a new and negative element will be added to the lore of cost accounting. Environmental demands may very well give rise to joint costs involved specifically in the elimination of pollution caused by waste arising from the production of several products.

Split-off Point. The point at which products assume separate identities is known as the *split-off point.* Up to the split-off point there can be no separate identification of costs; all costs are joint-product costs until the products are separately identifiable. The split-off points for all the products that are derived from the same processing do not necessarily occur at the same time. Continuing with the example of the hog, the removal of the hide is a split-off point only for the hide and bristles; these in turn go through a separate joint-product processing until the bristles are removed from the hide. The meat and bone products have other split-off points.

Incremental Costs. *Incremental costs* are those costs incurred after the last split-off point. When the hide becomes the final identifiable product, all subsequent costs incurred in tanning and curing are incremental costs. By their very nature incremental costs can be charged to the product and are specifically identified with it.

ACCOUNTING FOR JOINT-PRODUCT COSTS

By definition, joint-product costs are costs attributable to two or more products that contribute significant amounts to total sales. To say that pork chops cost more to produce than hide bristles places a cost on each in terms of how one values each individually. However, there is no way of knowing what the costs of the individual parts of the hog are. Insofar as these individual costs are concerned, planning and controlling are not possible. In spite of the fact that costs cannot be known, some rational figures are necessary both for financial statement purposes and for satisfying the requirements of certain governmental regulatory agencies. Several methods are used to help develop the numbers.

Sales-Value Method. Probably the most generally used method of assigning inventory values to joint products is to value them in proportion to their respective sales values at the time of split-off. This method is illustrated in Figure 6.1. Assume that both the hide and the carcass have a sales value at the time of split-off. The total costs are allocated to each product on the basis of their relative sales value, one-third for hide and two-thirds for carcass.

Sales value		
Hide	$ 5	(⅓)
Carcass	10	(⅔)
Total sales value	$15	
Costs to split-off point $6		
Hide	$ 2	(⅓)
Carcass	4	(⅔)
Total costs	$ 6	

Figure 6.1. Sales-value method

Relative-Weight Method. If the relative weight of the products at the split-off point has any significance, proportioning using weights instead of sales values can be done. Obviously, this method would have hardly any relevance in the case of the hog. If such a method is used, the units of measurement must be the same and must have some meaningful relation to each other.

Sales-Value-Minus-Cost-of-Completion Method. A variation of the sales-value method calls for the assignment of costs on the ratio of final selling prices, minus the costs of completion. Figure 6.2 illustrates this method. Assume that a processed hide sold for $10, and that incremental costs on the hide were $4. Also assume that the processed carcass sold for $20 and that incremental costs were $6. Costs are assigned as follows in Figure 6.2. (Notice that only the joint costs are subject to pro rata treatment. The incremental costs are allocated directly to the product incurring them.)

Realizable-Price Method. No matter which method is used, a good deal of work can be expended for nothing. Accordingly, some companies, particularly in the packing industry, merely value their inventory at market prices. This practice is subject to the objection that profits are anticipated; that is, if the $6 hog is valued at $15 (Figure 6.1), profits are being recorded on unsold goods. Certainly the packing industry has a valid re-

	Total	Hide	Carcass
Sales price	$30	$10	$20
Incremental costs	10	4	6
Sales price, less incremental cost	$20	$ 6	$14

Costs	Total	Hide	Carcass
Hog joint costs	$ 6	$1.80 (6/20 of $6)	$ 4.20 (14/20 of $6)
Incremental costs	10	4.00	6.00
Allocated costs	$16	$5.80	$10.20

Figure 6.2. Sales-value-minus-cost-of-completion method

joinder in that its turnover of inventory is so high and its inventory so readily salable that less harm is done by their practice than by the recording of conjectural figures. There is another way to meet the profit anticipation argument; namely, to value the inventory at its sales price and then reduce that figure by historic gross profit margins.

JOINT-PRODUCT COSTS AND MANAGEMENT

Management cannot make decisions based on joint-product costs arrived at in any of the ways illustrated above. It can, however, make decisions on whether or not incremental costs should be incurred. Returning to Figure 6.2, the illustrative case sets a sales price of $10 for a processed hide compared to $5 for an unprocessed hide. As long as processing costs are less than $5, there is a profit in processing. This is true whether or not the arbitrary method of assigning costs to the unprocessed hide indicates a cost of more or less than $5 for the unprocessed hide. The decision is (or should be) based on the difference between incremental revenues and incremental costs, not on the difference between total revenues and total assigned costs.

JOINT-PRODUCT COSTS AND GOVERNMENTAL REGULATION

Some joint-product costs are subject to governmental regulation, most notably in the oil and gas industry. A sizable percentage of oil wells are also a source of marketable natural gas. The price of natural gas moving in interstate commerce is subject to regulation by the Federal Power Commission; the price of petroleum is not. The price at which natural gas can be sold depends on its cost and the cost of transmission. The cost of transmission is, of course, an incremental cost and does not help to determine how much cost is properly applied to each product.

The price method cannot be used because the price depends on the cost, which, if fixed upon the price, leaves us right back where we started. Other methods, such as using the number of British thermal units in each product, have been suggested. A method frequently used by the Federal Power Commission is to assign costs to products as if these costs were incurred in wells that produce a single product, that is, only gas or oil.

Another problem encountered in joint-product costs is setting inventory values acceptable to the Internal Revenue Service. It is elementary accounting that the greater the closing inventory values set on the same quantity of goods, the higher the profit. The problem with the IRS would normally occur only in the first year joint-products appear in inventory. Thereafter, there would only be insistence on uniform treatment at the end of each subsequent year. The official Treasury view, which is not in any way binding on other federal agencies, is found in Section 1.471-3(d) of the income-tax regulations:

In any industry in which the usual rules for computation of cost of production are inapplicable, costs may be approximated upon such basis as may be reasonable and in conformity with established trade practice in the particular industry. Among such cases are: (1) farmers and raisers of livestock (see 1.471–6); (2) miners and manufacturers who by a single process or uniform series of processes derive a product of two or more kinds, sizes, or grades, the unit cost of which is substantially alike (see 1.471–7); and (3) retail merchants who use what is known as the "retail method" in ascertaining approximate cost (see 1.471–8).

ACCOUNTING FOR BY-PRODUCTS

As a practical matter, it may be difficult to determine whether a particular physical result of the manufacturing process should be classified as a joint product or a by-product. Even though the distinction may not be clear-cut for purposes of definition, once defined there is a considerable difference in accounting treatment. No costs are assigned to by-products. Revenues from their sale are treated either as reductions of costs or as other income. In fact, there are many different ways to handle the sale of by-products on the income statement.

By-product Revenues in the Income Statement. The data below are manipulated in Figures 6.3 through 6.8 to show the six most commonly used methods of handling the sale of by-products on the income statement.

Sales		$100,000
Production costs		75,000
Closing inventory		15,000
Sales of by-product	$1,500	
Less: Cost of disposal	500	1,000
Unsold by-product		300
Cost of disposal of unsold by-product		100
Sales		$100,000
Cost of goods sold		
Production costs	$75,000	
Less: Closing inventory	15,000	60,000
Gross profit		40,000
Other income		
By-product sales, net		1,000
Gross profit and other income		$ 41,000

Figure 6.3. By-product sales treated as other income*

* Under this method the market value of the ending inventory of unsold by-product is disregarded in computing profits.

Sales		$100,000
Cost of goods sold		
Production costs	$75,000	
Less: Closing inventory	15,000	
	60,000	
Less: By-product sales, net	1,000	59,000
Gross profit		$ 41,000

*Figure 6.4. By-product sales treated as a reduction of cost**

* By-product sales are treated as a reduction of cost of sales. Unsold by-product is disregarded in computing profits.

Sales		$100,000
Cost of goods sold		
Production costs	$75,000	
Less: By-product sales, net	1,000	
	74,000	
Less: Closing inventory	15,000	59,000
Gross profit		$41,000

*Figure 6.5. By-product sales treated as a reduction of production costs**

* Unsold by-product values are disregarded.

Sales, including by-product		$101,000
Cost of goods sold		
Production costs	$75,000	
Less: closing inventory	15,000	60,000
Gross profit		$ 41,000

*Figure 6.6. By-product sales treated as sales income**

* Unsold by-product values are disregarded.

Figures 6.3 through 6.8 demonstrate that, since there is more than one way to skin a hog, a company should be sure that all its divisions are handling these costs in the same manner if it wishes to make comparisons.

By-product Reused in Processing. In some industries, by-products can be recycled back into the production process. One

Sales			$100,000
Cost of goods sold			
Production costs		$75,000	
Less: Closing inventory		15,000	
		60,000	
Less: realizable value of by-product		1,200*	58,800
Gross profit			$ 41,200

```
* Realizable value of by-product;
    Sold                                    $1,500
    Unsold                                     300
                                             1,800
    Less: Costs to sell
       Sold                       $500
       Unsold                      100       600
    Realizable value of by-product           $1,200
```

Figure 6.7. Realizable value of by-product treated as a reduction of production costs

Sales			$100,000
Cost of goods sold			
Production costs		$75,000	
Realizable value of by-product		1,200	
		73,800	
Less: Closing inventory		14,960*	58,840
Gross profit			$ 41,160

```
* The closing inventory is reduced by the salable value of by-product:
    Realizable value of by-product        1,200
                                         ------- = 1.6%
    Production costs                      75,000

    Closing inventories                  $15,000
       Less: 1.6%                            240
                                          14,760
    Add: Sales value of by-product           200
    Closing inventory                    $14,960
```

Figure 6.8. Realizable value of by-product treated as a reduction of the cost of production and closing inventory

example is the gas generated in the manufacture of coke. This gas can be recycled and used to heat the ovens for manufacture of more coke and gas. Another example is pigged metal in a specialty foundry. In both cases, the by-product is both salable and reusable. Where the gas is recycled to the oven, the cost of the main product or joint product is automatically credited because no additional costs are incurred. In the case of the foundry, however, it would be most logical to charge stores inventory for the purchase price of similar metal and credit the process for the value. This is similar to one of the generally used methods to account for scrap that is discussed further in chapter 7.

Scrap and Spoiled Production

A manufacturing system that made ideal use of its raw materials would leave no residue from manufacturing, and each item of production would be perfect. Unfortunately, labor costs in such a system might well be prohibitive. Many manufacturing systems recognize that the additional costs to achieve perfection or near perfection are unwarranted. Therefore, some materials which are injected into the production process are deliberately not part of the final production. Human error, of course, also accounts for substantial scrap and spoiled production.

SCRAP

Scrap is that material which is deliberately left over after some part of the manufacturing process has been completed. Examples of scrap are the remainder of a strip of metal from which parts have been punched and the heads and gates in standard foundry practice. Furthermore, scrap by definition has a value over and above its costs of disposal and must be recognized in the accounting system.

Job-Order System. Where scrap can be traced to a specific job order, the cost of that job order should be credited with the value of the scrap, less disposal costs. The entry would be:

<blockquote>
Stores
    Work in process—Job number
</blockquote>

or

<blockquote>
Cash
    Cost of sales—Job number
</blockquote>

This treatment is of particular importance where the scrap is of relatively high value compared with the total of material costs charged to a given job order. Where the scrap is of a relatively low comparative value, for example, machine turnings, or where the correlation of scrap with a particular job order is not feasible, the value of or price received for the scrap is credited to departmental overhead:

> Stores
>> Departmental overhead

> or

> Cash
>> Departmental overhead

The price of scrap may fluctuate widely. Where this is true, the general practice is to credit overhead with a nominal amount when returning scrap to stores or to delay the credit to departmental overhead until the scrap is sold. When operations are at a substantially even level from period to period this practice has much to commend it pragmatically because only the first and last periods of operation would suffer from a reporting distortion.

Standard-Cost System. When scrap is a significant factor it should be considered in determining the standard. If, for example, 1,600 one-pound pieces are stamped from one ton of steel, the standard materials usage per unit of production, even though the unit weighs only one pound, should be 1.25 pounds. The cost standard will be either the cost of 1.25 pounds of steel or that figure less the value assigned to the scrap.

Special steel per ton	$600
Less: Value of scrap	
(400 pounds @ $120 per ton)	24
Standard cost of 1,600 pieces	$576

$$\frac{\$576}{1,600 \text{ pieces}} = \$0.36 \text{ Standard cost per unit}$$

If the assignment of scrap to a particular item produced is not feasible, the value of the scrap can be credited to departmental overhead as in a job-order system. If the value is significant, the value of the scrap itself might become a standard.

DEFECTIVE PRODUCTION

Units of production that do not meet quality control standards are *defective production*. Such material is frequently called scrap and is very often scrapped, but for control purposes it should not be confused with the planned nonuse of raw materials, which has been defined above as scrap. The important question in connection with defective materials is whether or not they should be reworked. If $1,000 has already been expended on a batch that did not meet quality control standards, but the batch could be sold for $100, it makes no economic sense to rework the batch at an additional cost of $500 and then sell it for $550.

	Sell Scrap
Costs to date	$1,000
Sales as scrap	100
Loss	$ 900

	Rework Scrap
Cost to date	$1,000
Rework costs	500
	$1,500
Sale as seconds	550
Loss	$ 950

While the above is simple and logical, actual practice is much more complex. First, in deciding whether or not to rework, the costs to date and the costs of reworking may be unknown. Second, it is a natural human tendency to hope that the rework costs "won't be too much" or that they can be hidden in connection with the results for the whole accounting period. This is particularly true when the alternative is the embarrassment of seeing units being physically hauled away to the scrap heap. Accordingly, many firms simply do not permit rework and require the scrapping of materials that do not meet quality standards at inspection points.

If, however, rework is undertaken, the accounting treatment for the amounts spent varies widely. The usual practice is to charge rework costs to departmental overhead. This is theoretically unsound if full absorption costing is used because it results in relatively higher overhead rates and increases the cost of all units, including those to which no value was added by the rework. Charging a particular job order for the rework is also unsound because the extra costs charged, plus the original costs, are not a true measure of the value of the product as long as it remains in inventory. Probably the best practice is to charge an account called simply "rework costs" and to close that account out monthly to the cost of goods manufactured.

WASTE

Waste is that part of the raw materials introduced into the production process that does not become part of the final product and that, because it has no value, cannot be sold as scrap. Obviously, waste may have a negative cost impact because its disposal is expensive. The cost of disposing of ash, sludge, slag, smoke, and so forth is part of the cost of the product. When these costs can be traced to a particular operation or process, they should be assigned as part of departmental overhead; otherwise, they are part of general manufacturing overhead. When waste is simply dumped into public waters or the air, its costs become a social cost. The public is subsidizing the costs of products that pollute our natural resources, but such social costs do not yet appear on the company's books.

Accounting for the shrinkage represented by waste is the same as accounting for scrap whether a job-order or a standard-cost system is used, except that there is no anticipated revenue. Waste or shrinkage may itself be expressed as a standard. For example, if 5 percent of the material input is lost through evaporation, a 95 percent yield would be the material usage standard.

SPOILED PRODUCTION

Spoiled production is the same as defective production except that it is disposed of rather than reworked.

Job-Cost System. Spoiled production is a normal expectation in most manufacturing processes. The usual practice, therefore, is to credit work in process with the salvage value of the spoiled production. If the quantity of spoiled production is normal, this practice spreads its costs over the good production and is not objectionable. However, when the quantity of spoiled production is abnormal, the abnormality should be charged to a separate account and closed each month to the cost of goods manufactured. Figure 7.1 illustrates the different possible results that the differing practices would achieve.

Total costs to manufacture		$50,000
Units started		5,000
"Normal" spoiled units		500
Actual spoiled units		1,000
Salvage value per spoiled unit		$ 1
Unit costs:		
No spoiled production	($50,000 ÷ 5,000)	$ 10
"Normal" spoiled production	($49,500 ÷ 4,500)	11
"Abnormal" spoiled production	($49,000 ÷ 4,000)	12.25

Figure 7.1. Comparison of methods of accounting for spoiled production

The argument against using a unit cost of $12.25 is that as long as any units remain in inventory, an expense of this accounting period, that is, the cost of the abnormal spoilage, will be deferred until a subsequent accounting period when the units have been sold. The preferred practice would carry 4,000 units into inventory at $11 each and charge the remaining $5,000 ($50,000 costs less $44,000 inventory and $1,000 salvage) to cost of goods manufactured in the accounting period in which the spoiled units were generated.

Standard-Cost System. The standard cost for the goods produced in Figure 7.1 would be $11. The abnormal spoilage could be analyzed as a separate variance, illustrated in Figure 7.2. Figure 7.2 uses the same facts as Figure 7.1 except that actual manufacturing costs are shown as $51,000 before deducting the amounts realized as salvage.

	Standard	Actual
Materials	$12,500	$12,500
Labor	12,500	13,125
Fixed overhead	12,500	12,500
Variable overhead	12,500	12,875
	$50,000	$51,000
Sale of spoiled units	500	1,000
	$49,500	$50,000
Units produced	4,500	4,000

Variance Analysis

	Spoiled	Other	Total
Direct material	$1,375		$1,375
Labor	1,375	$ 625	2,000
Fixed overhead	1,375		1,375
Variable overhead	1,375	375	1,750
Sale of spoiled units	(500)		(500)
	$5,000	$1,000	$6,000

Figure 7.2. *Variance analysis of abnormal spoiled production*

Process-Cost System. The problems in connection with spoiled production are usually encountered in manufacturing companies that employ process-cost systems. Since process-cost concepts can be utilized by companies using either a standard-cost system or other cost systems, no problems are encountered other than those presented above.

SPOILAGE RATE BASE: INPUT OR OUTPUT? If the practice is to charge abnormal spoiled production to a special account, the question of the base for determining normal spoiled production arises. In Figures 7.1 and 7.2 it was assumed that normal spoiled production is 10 percent of the input; that is, input is for 5,000 units and normal good production is 4,500 units. In theory it would be more accurate to express normal spoiled production as 11.11 percent of good units produced (500 spoiled units ÷ 4,500 good units). When only 4,000 units are produced, it follows that normal spoiled production is 444 units, rather than the 500 shown in Figure 7.2. The variance analysis shown in Figure 7.2 would be restated as follows:

	Spoiled	Other	Total
Direct materials	$1,526		$1,526
Labor	1,526	$ 248	1,774
Fixed overhead	1,526		1,526
Variable overhead	1,526	148	1,674
Sale of spoiled units	(444)*	(56)	(500)
	$5,660	$ 340	$6,000

* Figures rounded.

SPOILAGE RATE BASE: NORMAL RATE OF SPOILAGE. While it is convenient to use a normal spoiled production rate of 10 or 11.11 percent based on past experience, the actual rate of spoiled production will probably vary from month to month. When this occurs, control is probably better served by reporting all spoiled production as variances, that is, not recognizing a normal rate. Some companies maintain an account similar to over- and under-absorbed overhead for the monthly deviations from the anticipated normal rate of spoiled production.

SPOILED PRODUCTION: EQUIVALENT UNITS. Unless spoiled production occurs evenly throughout the process, as might be the case with evaporation, the question arises whether or not the spoiled production should be used in computing the cost of equivalent units. Figure 7.3 illustrates the consequences of including or excluding the spoiled production from the equivalent unit base. It is assumed that the weighted-average method of computing equivalent units is used so that the units and costs from the previous accounting period are included in the totals.

Beginning inventory	5,000 units	½ completed
Transferred in	10,000 units	
Spoiled production	1,500 units	
Transferred out	11,000 units	
Ending inventory	2,500 units	⅕ completed
Total costs	$29,900	

First assumption: Spoiled production excluded from base
  Equivalent units:

Beginning inventory	5,000 units
Started and completed	6,000
Ending inventory (⅕ of 2,500)	500
	11,500 units

Unit cost	$29,900 ÷ 11,500 =	$2.60	
11,000 Units @ $2.60		$28,600	
500 Equivalent units @ $2.60		1,300	
		$29,900	

Second assumption: Spoiled production included in base
  Equivalent units:

Beginning inventory	5,000 units
Started and completed	6,000
Spoiled production	1,500
Ending inventory (⅕ of 2,500)	500
	13,000 units

Unit cost	$29,900 ÷ 13,000 =	$2.30	
11,000 Units @ $2.30			$25,300
1,500 Spoiled units @ $2.30			3,450
500 Equivalent units @ $2.30			1,150
			$29,900

Figure 7.3. Consequences of excluding spoiled production from equivalent units

CHAPTER 8

Problems in Overhead Allocation

This chapter completes the discussion of the allocation of over-head to various departments and products that was begun earlier.

DEPARTMENTAL VERSUS COMPANY-WIDE RATES

If there is no difference in the processing of several products in different departments of a factory, company-wide rates are cheaper and easier to use than departmental rates, and calculations are greatly simplified. However, if, as is usually the case, there are differences both in the amount of overhead incurred in individual departments and in the amount of processing by each department on different products, departmental rates would more clearly show the cost of individual products. For example, assume that a company manufactures ornamental flowerpots. Some of the flowerpots are decorated by hand and sell at high prices; others are stenciled by machine and are more moderately priced. Obviously, the hand decorating department is labor-intensive and has a relatively low rate of overhead using labor hours or dollars as a base. The situation in the stenciling department is the reverse, yet on a company-wide basis, both products would be charged with the same overhead rate. In practice, departmental rates are usually more appropriate than company-wide rates.

Control Factors of Overhead Rates. One of the most difficult problems in the allocation of overhead rates from a service department to another department is the assessment of who controls such overhead costs, the using department or the service department. The most logical answer would be both. The user would determine the quantity of such services used, while the supplier would determine their quality. Most companies solve the problem by assigning responsibility to the using department for its actual use at some standard unit cost. As a result of this practice, the using department is primarily responsible for the quantity of service, and the service department, for quality and cost control. This system works particularly well with flexible budgeting as discussed in chapter 9.

An example of control over overhead is derived from an actual occurrence in a manufacturing company. The sales department would come in with a rush order. Because of the rush order, the production department was forced to work overtime. This happened many, many times, and the production department felt that it was being penalized in its reported performance because of the additional costs resulting from overtime. After negotiation, enforced by higher management, it was agreed that the production department would process all normal orders at standard rates but that the sales department would be charged for any overtime caused by rush orders. As might be expected, the demand for rush orders fell drastically.

Other control problems arise because some costs allocated to departments are not controllable by the department. For example, the factory manager's salary may, in part, be allocated to the machine shop so that full costs can be allocated to all products machined. It is necessary to know what all costs are for purposes of product costing and the financial statements. However, it is not wise to report costs over which he has no control to a manager. Other problems, of course, stem from reporting figures that are less than total. It is not difficult to develop subsidiary control totals to avoid these problems.

BASES FOR ALLOCATION

By its very nature, overhead cannot be traced to individual products. The inability to trace overhead to units of production leads to several problems in allocation, including the choice of an appropriate allocation base, the choice of a reasonable allocation method, and the determination of product cost.

Physical Units Produced. One of the more obvious bases for the allocation of overhead is physical units produced. Under this method, divide total overhead by total units produced to find the overhead rate to be allocated. This basis of allocation becomes especially attractive when the units produced are homogeneous. The units produced, of course, pertain to the physical production of that particular department. A payroll department, for example, might allocate its costs on the total number of paychecks written. This method is also particularly advantageous in a process-type operation.

Direct-Labor Hours or Direct-Labor Cost. Many firms allocate overhead on the basis of either direct-labor hours or total direct-labor cost. As long as labor rates are fairly uniform, both methods will yield the same dollar allocation. However, if there is a substantial variation between the wage rates of skilled labor and unskilled labor, serious distortion can be caused by the use of direct-labor cost instead of direct-labor hours in allocating total overhead. To determine which method is more appropriate, an examination should be made of the type of overhead charges being allocated. If fixed overhead costs are a substantial portion of total overhead and these fixed overhead costs are time-related, for example, supervisory salaries, the passage of time as expressed in direct-labor hours would be the more appropriate divisor. On the other hand, if the overhead arises from fringe benefits paid to labor, which are a function of direct-labor costs, direct-labor dollar costs would be an appropriate allocation base. A paper-work flow would have to be devised to charge such costs to specific products. Overhead rates would be computed by dividing total overhead by either expected total direct-labor hours or expected total direct-labor costs, depending on the base chosen. The overhead cost of any given operation or product would then be determined by multiplying the derived overhead rate by the number of hours or the number of dollars spent on direct labor for that operation or product.

Machine Hours. Labor hours and costs are most frequently used as the basis for allocating overhead because they are already collected for payroll purposes, and very little additional clerical effort is required to produce the information needed to use them as an overhead base. As production is automated, however, labor costs become an increasingly smaller portion of total costs. The operating costs of the machines and their amortization is quite often a substantial multiple of total direct-labor costs. While it is often difficult to accumulate information on the machine hours utilized on a particular job, this objection becomes less valid as the mechanical operations become controlled by computers, which have the technological capability of accumulating the necessary information at little or no extra cost. To use machine hours as the basis for allocating overhead cost, divide total overhead by the expected machine hours to be expended during a normal time period, and multiply the quotient by the number of machine hours used on any individual job.

Material Weight or Material Cost. Material weight or material cost is occasionally used as a basis for allocation of overhead. In this method the total overhead budgeted for a period is divided by the weight or cost anticipated for a normal period and then allocated on the basis of the total weight or total cost, whichever basis is being used. In most situations, material weight or material cost would not be a good index for allocating overhead. However, where its use would result in no significant difference and it is more convenient, it could be employed. The necessary information would come from the storeroom tickets charging out the material to a job either by weight or by cost. The use of material weight or cost as an overhead base would ordinarily be restricted to a job order cost system.

Floor Space and Other Bases of Overhead Allocation. There are many other bases for allocation of overhead besides those mentioned above. One of the most common is floor space. Floor space is a particularly useful basis when a major portion of overhead comes from depreciation and maintenance costs and where there is a relationship between the area involved in an operation and the cost applied. When these relationships do not hold true, floor space is a poor method to use to allocate overhead. As far as other methods are concerned, the essential point to remember is that any basis for the allocation of overhead to determine the profitability or efficiency of a particular department is acceptable as long as it does not distort reality. In fact, the prime consideration in allocation of overhead should be to use that basis which is easiest and/or least expensive to apply as long as there is little or no distortion of the cost of individual departments. Above all, it should be remembered that any system includes many arbitrary assumptions; thus, rigid adherence to past practices and assumptions may well be counterproductive.

SERVICE DEPARTMENTS AND PROBLEMS IN COST ALLOCATION

Frequently, there is an obvious but not directly measurable relationship between overhead and production. An example is the salary of the department foreman in a particular production department where the relationship between the salary of its foreman and the cost of all the products turned out by his department is clear, even though it is impossible to determine how much of his salary should be directly applicable to any one product. It is far more difficult, however, to see the relationship of the cost of a medical department or the cost of a company cafeteria to the production department and even more difficult to relate these costs to particular products. All products should carry their appropriate share of these costs. In order to meet the objective of assigning all costs to all products, the costs which occur in the service department must somehow be applied to production departments and from there directly to products. In the process, overhead rates that will encompass both the production and the service departments will be used. Returning to the earlier discussion of departmental versus company-wide rates, it is easy to see why, in this circumstance, departmental rates would be preferred.

The basis for allocating costs from service departments to other departments should be that which best measures the relative benefits received by all other departments. These allocations can be made on the basis of any of several modes of paperwork or information flow already used by management for other purposes.

Probably the most widely used criterion is ease of allocation. An example of this would be a situation that occurred several years ago at an oil refinery. In the attempt to determine the appropriate basis for applying pumping expenses to the various other departments of the refinery, several bases were considered. The basis finally chosen was hours of pumping because it was simple and the total dollar amount of the allocation was small. This basis was selected even though it was obvious that there were many areas in pumping where labor hours (including setup and knockdown time), size of pipes, and horsepower would have been a more accurate measure.

METHODS OF COST ALLOCATION

Once a company has selected a basis for allocation of costs for each department, it must select a procedure to follow in allocating the cost of a service department to a production department. The next few sections will discuss some of the more common procedures. A basic example will be used to demonstrate the various methods of allocation. The data for the illustrative examples are given in Figure 8.1.

After a careful examination of the situation shown in Figure 8.1, the Skider Corporation decided to allocate engineering costs on the basis of the hours of engineering assistance given to each division except engineering. It also decided to allocate maintenance cost on the basis of floor space required for each department except maintenance. Administrative costs were to be applied to all departments other than administration on the basis of their total number of employees.

Direct Allocation of Overhead Costs to Revenue-Producing Departments. The most widely used method of applying overhead costs from service departments to production departments is the direct allocation method. Under this method any charges for service rendered by a service department are allocated directly to producing departments. Using the facts of Figure 8.1, the only hours considered in allocating engineering overhead would be the 3,000 hours each in machining, assembling, and finishing. The 500 engineering hours devoted to administration and maintenance would be ignored in allocating the $90,000 engineering costs. Similarly, in applying the maintenance costs the only floor space considered would be the 30,000 square feet in the ma-

SKIDER CORPORATION

	Service Departments			Production Departments		
	Administration	Maintenance	Engineering	Machining	Assembling	Finishing
Overhead costs incurred	$240,000	$180,000	$90,000	$300,000	$500,000	$400,000
Number of employees	10	15	5	15	20	25
Square feet of floor space required	12,500	2,000	12,500	30,000	40,000	30,000
Hours of engineering directly rendered	500	500	1,000	3,000	3,000	3,000
Machine hours				80,000		
Direct labor hours					100,000	50,000

Figure 8.1. Cost allocation data

chinery department, 40,000 in the assembling department, and 30,000 in the finishing department. In allocating administrative costs the only employees considered would be the 15, 20, and 25 in machining, assembling, and finishing respectively.

Figure 8.2 demonstrates the direct method of reapportionment.

Single-Step Method of Allocation. While the direct allocation of service department costs to production departments, ignoring services performed for other service departments, has the virtue of simplicity and ease of computation, it can be highly misleading. This is especially true if the department receiving services has a significantly different base for distributing costs to producing departments than the one rendering service. The differences produced by the example of the Skider Corporation are probably not significant, which illustrates the pragmatic point that it is frequently necessary to make a computation to determine that it need not be made.

Figure 8.3 demonstrates the use of the single-step method of overhead allocation using the information set forth in Figure 8.1. The major distinction between the direct method and the single-step method illustrated in Figure 8.3 is in the allocation of service department costs. In Figure 8.3 administrative costs are allocated on the basis of the number of employees in each department other than administration. Since there are 80 such employees, each department receives as its share of the $240,000 cost of administration, the number of its employees divided by 80 rather than by 60 as in Figure 8.2. Similar procedures are followed for maintenance and engineering, with the exception that as a department is closed-out, it is not charged with the cost of any other service department's costs.

Double-Step Method of Allocation. A more equitable reapportionment of overhead costs is obtained under the single-step method of allocation illustrated in Figure 8.3 than under the direct method illustrated in Figure 8.2 because the services rendered between service departments are partly taken into consideration. To achieve even greater recognition of this logic, many companies use a double-step method. This method is widely used by nursing homes in applying for cost reimbursement under Medicare and Medicaid programs.

SKIDER CORPORATION

	Administration	Maintenance	Engineering	Machinery	Assembling	Finishing
Overhead costs before allocation	$240,000	$180,000	$90,000	$300,000	$500,000	$400,000
First step:						
Allocation of administration						
15/60, 20/60, 25/60*	(240,000)			60,000	80,000	100,000
Second step:						
Allocation of maintenance						
30,000/100,000						
40,000/100,000						
30,000/100,000†		(180,000)		54,000	72,000	54,000
Third step:						
Allocation of engineering						
3,000/9,000						
3,000/9,000						
3,000/9,000‡			(90,000)	30,000	30,000	30,000
Total overhead of producing departments				$444,000	$682,000	$584,000
To compute overhead rates for product costing:						
Divide by machine hours				80,000		
Divide by direct labor hours					100,000	50,000
Rate				$ 5.55	$ 6.82	$ 11.68

* Base is (15 + 20 + 25) = 60 employees.
† Base is (30,000 + 40,000 + 30,000) = 100,000 square feet.
‡ Base is (3,000 + 3,000 + 3,000) = 9,000 man-hours.

Figure 8.2. Direct method of allocation

89

SKIDER CORPORATION

	Administration	Maintenance	Engineering	Machinery	Assembling	Finishing
Overhead costs before allocation	$240,000	$180,000	$ 90,000	$300,000	$500,000	$400,000
First step:						
Allocation of administration						
15/80, 5/80, 15/80, 20/80,						
25/80*	($240,000)	45,000	15,000	45,000	60,000	75,000
Second step:						
Allocation of maintenance						
12,500/112,500						
30,000/112,500						
40,000/112,500						
30,000/112,500†		($225,000)	25,000	60,000	80,000	60,000
Third step:						
Allocation of Engineering						
3,000/9,000						
3,000/9,000						
3,000/9,000‡			($130,000)	43,333	43,333	43,334
Total overhead of producing departments				$448,333	$683,333	$578,334
To compute overhead rates for product costing:						
Divide by machine hours				80,000		
Divide by direct labor hours					100,000	50,000
Rate				$ 5.6042	$ 6.8333	$11.5667

* Base is (15 + 5 + 15 + 20 + 25) = 80 employees.
† Base is (12,500 + 30,000 + 40,000 + 30,000) = 112,500 square feet.
‡ Base is (3,000 + 3,000 + 3,000) = 9,000 man-hours.

Figure 8.3. Single-step method of allocation

90

The double-step method has greater validity than the single-step method because in the first step all service department expenses are allocated to all other departments. After this first allocation, the remaining costs are allocated as in the single-step method. An example is given in Figure 8.4.

Multiple-Equation Approach to Overhead Allocation. The development of single- and double-step methods leads to the logical conclusion that the most sophisticated technique for allocation of overhead between service and producing departments would be one in which all reciprocal relationships are expressed. This can be done by developing a series of equations to represent the apportionment of service cost from each department to every other department. The reciprocal relationships for the Skider Corporation are shown in Figure 8.5.

The percentages used in Figure 8.5 are based on the relationships expressed in Figure 8.1. For example, to derive percentages for administration, find the total number of employees in all departments other than administration—80 employees. Use 80 as the denominator and the number of employees in maintenance as the numerator to determine the proper fraction to be allocated to maintenance ($15 \div 80$). Converting $15 \div 80$ to percentages yields 18.75 percent. Repeat this process for each department to calculate Figure 8.5.

The allocation to production and service department percentages developed in Figure 8.5 can be expressed in equation form when combined with the preallocation total overhead costs. In the following equations, X_1 represents administration; X_2, maintenance; X_3, engineering; X_4, machining; X_5, assembling; and X_6, finishing.

$$
\begin{aligned}
(1)\quad X_1 &= 240{,}000 + .1000X_2 + .0500X_3 \\
(2)\quad X_2 &= 180{,}000 + .1875X_1 + .0500X_3 \\
(3)\quad X_3 &= 90{,}000 + .0625X_1 + .1000X_2 \\
(4)\quad X_4 &= 300{,}000 + .1875X_1 + .2400X_2 + .3000X_3 \\
(5)\quad X_5 &= 500{,}000 + .2500X_1 + .3200X_2 + .3000X_3 \\
(6)\quad X_6 &= 400{,}000 + .3125X_1 + .2400X_2 + .3000X_3
\end{aligned}
$$

The above equations express the total cost of each department as a function of its direct dollar overhead cost plus its share of

	Administration	Maintenance	Engineering	Machining	Assembling	Finishing
Overhead costs before allocation	$240,000	$180,000	$90,000	$300,000	$500,000	$400,000
First step:						
1st Allocation of Admin.*	(240,000)	45,000	15,000	45,000	60,000	75,000
1st Allocation of Maint.†		(225,000)	22,500	54,000	72,000	54,000
1st Allocation of Engin.‡		6,375	(127,500)	38,250	38,250	38,250
Second step:						
2d Allocation of Admin.§	(28,875)	5,414	1,805	5,414	7,219	9,023
2d Allocation of Maint.§		(11,789)	1,310	3,144	4,191	3,144
2d Allocation of Engin.§			(3,115)	1,038	1,039	1,038
Total overhead of producing departments				$446,846	$682,699	$580,455
To compute overhead rates for product costing						
Divide by machine hours				80,000		
Divide by direct labor hours					100,000	50,000
Rate				$5.5856	$6.8290	$11.6091

* Base for allocation is (15 + 5 + 15 + 20 + 25) = 80 employees.
† Base for allocation is (12,500 + 12,500 + 30,000 + 40,000 + 30,000) = 125,000 square feet.
‡ Base for allocation is (500 + 500 + 3,000 + 3,000 + 3,000) = 10,000 labor hours.
§ Use the same base for allocation as in Figure 8.3.

Figure 8.4. Double-step method of allocation

SERVICE DEPARTMENT ALLOCATION TO PRODUCTION AND SERVICE DEPARTMENTS

	Total	Administration (X_1)	Maintenance (X_2)	Engineering (X_3)	Machining (X_4)	Assembling (X_5)	Finishing (X_6)
Administration	100%	—	18.75%	6.25%	18.75%	25.00%	31.25%
Maintenance	100%	10.00%	—	10.00%	24.00%	32.00%	24.00%
Engineering	100%	5.00%	5.00%	—	30.00%	30.00%	30.00%

Figure 8.5. Calculation of allocation percentages for multiple-equation approach

the costs allocated from other departments. To solve this problem, first solve equations (1), (2), and (3) for X_1, X_2, and X_3. Then substitute the solved values into equations 4 through 6. Solving these equations would yield the following costs for machining, assembling, and finishing.

	Machining	Assembling	Finishing
Total allocated and direct costs	$446,784	$682,651	$580,565
To compute overhead rate for product costing			
Divide by machine hours	80,000		
Divide by direct labor hours		100,000	50,000
Rate	$ 5.5848	$ 6.8265	$11.6113

The same results can be derived simply by substituting the arithmetic values of X_1, X_2, . . . X_6 and manually cycling these amounts until X_1, X_2, and X_3 all equal zero. This is a simple approach and is frequently employed. Another technique that could be used is matrix algebra. With the increased adoption of computerized accounting systems and "canned" programs for solving matrix problems this technique is becoming more widely used, particularly where there are more than three reciprocal transfers of interdepartmental service expenses.

Comparison of the Four Approaches. As can be seen from Figure 8.6, there would be a different product cost and, assuming that product costs affect selling prices, a different selling price for each department. Although the differences in these examples are small, they can be very important for price setting.

		Department	
Method	Machining	Assembling	Finishing
Direct	$5.5500	$6.8200	$11.6800
Single-step	5.6042	6.8333	11.5667
Double-step	5.5856	6.8270	11.6091
Multiple-equation	5.5848	6.8265	11.6113

Figure 8.6. Comparison of product cost using various overhead allocation techniques

CAPACITY VERSUS USAGE IN ALLOCATING OVERHEAD

All the techniques demonstrated so far for the allocation of overhead treat overhead as an item to be apportioned on the basis of a single rate for each service department. Actually, for those companies using flexible budgeting (see chapter 9), it is more correct theoretically to allocate overhead using two rates. Each department should set up a rate based on the amount of service it is expected to provide based on the capacity demands of the departments it serves. Service departments should then allocate the fixed costs of providing their services on the basis of the representative share of the capacity demands of each of the user departments. The variable costs of providing services should be apportioned to the user departments on the basis of the actual use made of the facilities of the service department. Again, there is a problem in selecting an appropriate base of capacity measurement. Should the company choose ideal capacity, expected capacity, or normal capacity for the allocation of the fixed costs? See chapter 9 for a discussion of this problem.

Under a *dual-rate method* of overhead apportionment, the final allocation is determined after the completion of several steps.

1. Determine capacity required to service all departments at their period of peak demand.

2. Determine the cost of providing such services (possibly using regression analysis or other mathematical techniques to separate fixed from variable costs).

3. Allocate the fixed cost of providing capacity service to user departments on the basis of the capacity provided.

4. Determine the difference between the fixed and total costs.

5. Allocate these variable costs on the basis of actual service provided to the departments.

The classical example used to illustrate the dual-rate method is that of the power department in a manufacturing concern. Assume that one of the service departments at the Skider Corporation is a power service department that supplies horsepower

to the various other production and service departments as
follows:

SCHEDULING OF HORSEPOWER PROVIDED

	Total hours	Producing departments			Service departments	
		A	B	C	1	2
Required for capacity production	800,000	220,000	220,000	160,000	80,000	120,000
Actually used for year	600,000	180,000	150,000	150,000	30,000	90,000

It is determined that during the year the operating costs of the
power service department amounted to $320,000, of which
$200,000 was considered a fixed cost and the remaining $120,000
a variable cost. The $200,000 fixed cost should be considered the
cost of providing the ability to serve the other departments at
their capacity production and should be allocated on the basis
of capacity provided. The $120,000 variable cost should be allo-
cated on the basis of horsepower actually used. The dual-rate
allocation of the power service department costs is given in
Figure 8.7.

DEPARTMENT COSTS TO OTHER DEPARTMENTS ON A DUAL-RATE BASIS

	Total	A	B	C	1	2
Allocation of fixed costs:						
$.25 per hour of capacity provided ($200,000 ÷ 800,000 hours)	$200,000	$55,000	$55,000	$40,000	$20,000	$30,000
Allocation of variable costs:						
$.20 per hour used ($120,000 ÷ 600,000 hours)	120,000	36,000	30,000	30,000	6,000	18,000
Total Costs	$320,000	$91,000	$85,000	$70,000	$26,000	$48,000
Comparative allocation basis of capacity using						
$.40 single rate ($320,000 ÷ 800,000 hours)	$320,000	$88,000	$88,000	$64,000	$32,000	$48,000

Figure 8.7. Allocation of power service

CHAPTER 9

Budgeting

Budgeting serves a dual purpose. First, the budget is a plan of what is expected to happen. This plan can be formulated on either a cash receipts and disbursements basis or on an annual net profit basis, or both. At the same time, the budget serves as a target for performance on the part of all departments and individuals who make up the organization.

TECHNIQUE OF PERFORMANCE BUDGETING

A discussion of the subject of budgeting can start with either the theories or the techniques. However, a theory of budgeting based on unrealistic or unobtainable techniques is of little value. The preparation of a budget is a fairly simple mechanical process once a starting point is chosen.

Budget: A Pro Forma Financial Statement. In essence, a budget is merely a pro forma financial statement detailing the course of events anticipated for a given time period. (A pro forma financial statement is one which "would be" if given events had taken place.) The use of a budget is by no means confined to business. The federal budget is an enormously powerful tool in both the economy and the government. Other governmental units, schools, churches, and other nonbusiness organizations have found an increasing need to make financial plans for guidance in their operations.

BUDGETARY TIME PERIOD. Most frequently, budgets are prepared on the basis of the next fiscal year, subdivided into monthly or quarterly performance expectations. Unless the organization experiences relatively uniform activity during each calendar month, this is hardly a realistic approach except where adjustments are made for cyclical fluctuations. Furthermore, the months themselves are by no means the same units. It is entirely possible for the months of September and November to contain no more than nineteen working days while March, August, and October may contain as many as twenty-three. Often, quarters are the better periods for budgetary distinction, but they too should be adjusted if the business is at all cyclical.

Whatever period is adopted, it should include one major cycle of the firm's business. Many companies have both short- and long-range budget plans. A long-range plan is in a state of constant revision dependent on predictions as to the economy, new plant facilities, and new products. At the same time, more detailed plans are made each quarter for the quarter one year away. In this way, there is a constant one-year detailed budget at hand. Obviously, the quarter farthest away is the easiest to adjust for changes that may occur both within and outside the organization.

CASH BUDGET. Earlier it was pointed out that it is usually not the function of the cost accountant or the controller to provide the operating funds needed by the firm. However, it is proper to discuss cash budgeting at this point for two reasons. First, the cash budget is a necessary by-product of the sales-manufacturing plan. Furthermore, if funds to finance plans cannot be obtained, an attempt to carry through the plans might well be disastrous for the organization. Second, in many smaller firms the responsibility for managerial and financial accounting is combined. Then, again, in larger firms, budgeting may well be a responsibility in itself so that technical responsibility for both operating and financial budgets is combined in one budget executive.

A simplified format for a cash budget for several months is set forth in Figure 9.1.

Other techniques can be used in making cash budgets. Another frequently used technique is the pro forma statement of source and application of funds, more specifically, the schedule of changes in working capital that accompanies the statement. (See Figure 9.2.)

Projections. Budget projections are the first step in management's function of planning. The world may or may not beat a

	January	February	March	April	May
Cash Balance Beginning	$1,400,000	$1,525,000	$1,515,000	$ 355,000	$ 615,000
Receipts					
Dec. 31—Accounts receivable	1,200,000				
Jan. 31—Accounts receivable		150,000	50,000		
Feb. 28—Accounts receivable		1,000,000	185,000	65,000	75,000
Mar. 31—Accounts receivable			1,100,000	200,000	160,000
Apr. 30—Accounts receivable				1,050,000	1,400,000
Miscellaneous	25,000	10,000	15,000	30,000	15,000
Short-term borrowing			500,000		
Cash available	$2,625,000	$2,685,000	$3,365,000	$1,700,000	$2,265,000
Payments					
Dec. 31—Accounts payable	$ 650,000				
Jan. 31—Accounts payable		$ 700,000			
Feb. 28—Accounts payable			$2,185,000*		
Mar. 31—Accounts payable				$ 625,000	
Apr. 30—Accounts payable					$1,140,000†
Income tax (Mar. 15)			455,000		
Jan. wages & salaries	350,000				
Feb. wages & salaries		340,000			
Mar. wages & salaries			370,000		
Apr. wages & salaries				360,000	
May wages & salaries					350,000
Interest					130,000
Dividends	100,000	130,000		100,000	
Total Payments	$1,100,000	$1,170,000	$3,010,000	$1,085,000	$1,620,000
Balance	$1,525,000	$1,515,000	$ 355,000	$ 615,000	$ 645,000

* Includes installation of new machinery.
† Includes repayment of short-term borrowing.

Figure 9.1. Cash Budget

From operations:

Net income		$250,000
Add: Depreciation		75,000
Funds provided by operations		$325,000
Less: Dividends	$100,000	
Purchase of capital equipment	25,000	125,000
Net increase in working capital		$200,000

Schedule of changes in working capital

Cash increased	$150,000
Accounts receivable increased	75,000
Accounts payable decreased	25,000
	$250,000
Inventories decreased	50,000
Net increase	$200,000

Figure 9.2. Pro forma schedule of working capital changes

path to our door if we make better mousetraps. However, the question would remain: How many mousetraps does the world want? Before how much can be spent on production and marketing is determined, it is necessary to have some idea of how many units can be sold and at what price.

SALES FORECAST. Depending on the resources and sophistication of the firm, the sales forecast might well begin with the economist. In fact, if an economist is present in the firm, he is usually a member of the budget committee. In addition to the economy as a whole—and for some companies this might well embrace the economies of several countries—there remain questions as to the specific industry in which the firm or the particular product is involved. For example, during the latter years of the great economic boom of the 1960s, the private housing industry was considerably depressed. This affected not only builders but also manufacturers of housing hardware, appliances, and construction tools and machinery, among others.

Historical sales figures are an excellent guide to the future, but they certainly should not be the sole criterion. Furthermore, taking such figures in the abstract can be quite misleading. For example, a 25 percent increase in sales for a company would hardly be a matter for self-congratulation if sales in the industry had increased by 35 percent.

Perhaps the chief benefit of using historical figures is in evaluating the individual estimators themselves. Assume, for example, a situation where the firm relies on orders solicited by highly trained and motivated sales engineers, where the individual order may well involve several weeks' production. Some men are optimists; others, less sanguine. One of the principal problems of the coordinator of sales estimates may very well be the differences in reliability of the individual estimators.

In other firms, the problem may be that of estimating the sales of its customers (the so-called case of derived demand). Examine the problems of a company manufacturing specialty sheet steel for the appliance industry. Historical figures will give a pretty good idea of the steel firm's market "slice," but here the major question is someone else's market. In such a situation, it may be difficult to judge in advance the results to be obtained from an extensive advertising campaign. Nonetheless, such judgments are absolutely necessary.

Compounding all these problems are two more major unknowns. The first of these is technological. Reports of scientific breakthroughs are legion, along with extrapolations of what this may mean in terms of products. Judging when the breakthroughs become salable products in meaningful economic terms is a frustrating but frequently rewarding business. Then there is the problem of changing public taste. Whether the change in taste is a result of planned obsolescence or merely public satiation with a particular form of product is a matter of debate. One need only recall the large-car–compact-car swings in public taste during the 1960s to see the problem.

PROFIT FORECAST. Having decided with a good deal of trepidation what revenues are expected, it is then necessary to decide the firm's profit goals. This is a particularly important step for the multiproduct, multidivision company because anticipated profits are a major factor in deciding the allocation of resources. Within the individual divisions, it is also usual to project a desired profit, on the basis of either a percentage of sales or a percentage of capital invested.

Even where, because of economic and market conditions, no profit is expected, the loss should be budgeted. In terms of the long-term survival of the firm, it could be more important in one year to hold a loss within limits than to maximize profits. Additionally, where assets have been committed to a project and have become sunk costs, it might be more appropriate to budget a planned liquidation at a loss than to sell the assets for what they will bring or merely to halt production.

One of the best reasons for making a profit forecast along with the sales forecast is to have a thought-out guide with which to distinguish the possible from the desirable. Maximizing profit in a given year is not necessarily good business; by the same token many very desirable projects may simply be beyond the firm's means.

Manufacturing Budget. Having decided on sales and profit targets, the budgets for the production departments can be set. While it is always possible to substitute materials or to change production methods in order to save labor or overhead costs, a budget is established for the situation known to exist at the time.

Direct-Materials Budget. No matter how many products or divisions the company may have, at some point each product must be budgeted. Before labor can be expended, materials must be brought into the plant; furthermore, there must be a steady flow of materials for labor to work on. It is possible, of course, to lay off unneeded labor, but this is an expensive proposition even without regard to the social costs. Furthermore, the production lost by the failure to have materials on hand can frequently only be made up, if at all, through expensive overtime. Then, again, materials purchased on a crash basis are likely to cost more.

Note the figures for accounts payable in Figure 9.1. These arise from the purchase of everything the company uses—materials, supplies, capital goods, and so on. No projection for the cost of raw materials can be made without a prior determination of what the materials are, how much they cost, how much lead time is necessary for delivery, and the extent to which materials should be stocked.

It follows that the budget for raw material costs must be the joint product of the production, sales, scheduling, purchasing, cost, stores, and financial accounting departments. It would make little sense to budget for a lower unit price available for a quantity purchase of perishable items where there was no place to store them. If funds are available only at a prohibitive cost, optimum quantity purchases may not be possible.

Taking all these matters into consideration, a budget figure for raw materials is derived. For the firm, the figure will be a synthesis of the operating department figures.

DIRECT-LABOR BUDGET. As in the case of the direct-materials budget, the direct-labor budget affects many more managers in the company than the cost accountant or the departments where the labor is expended. If labor or particular skills are in short supply, the personnel department must know months in advance what requirements will be. If layoffs are anticipated, the personnel department may well need a good deal of lead time to make transfers dictated by a union contract or by reasons of economy.

Direct-labor budgets must be readjusted from time to time because of changes in product or means of production. It is probably wise to discuss readjustment in terms of hours rather than dollars. Sometimes the operating departments have control over the assignment of individual workers to tasks, which they do on the basis of wage rates. Frequently, however, union requirements set the rate for a task, and bumping procedures may temporarily result in a less efficient worker performing a task. As the result of cost-of-living union contracts, wage rates may change in the middle of a budget period. While dollar figures must be introduced into a financial plan, such as those set forth in Figures 9.1 and 9.2, they need not clutter up the planning for the amount of labor to be expended for a particular product.

OVERHEAD IN DIRECT-LABOR DEPARTMENTS. It is rare indeed for a manufacturing department to have no departmental overhead. In almost every department there are some expenditures that cannot be related to a particular product. Such expenditures may be for supervision, setup time, cleanup time, tool-repair time, power, supplies, and all the things besides direct materials and labor necessary to the performance of the departmental task. All expenditures in a particular direct-labor department that are not chargeable to direct labor or materials are departmental overhead. Normally, this overhead is charged only to work passing through the department. For example, it would be inaccurate and misleading to charge a product that was not plated with plating department overhead. It would be disastrous not to budget and control the overhead in a direct-labor department; otherwise budgets for direct labor could be charged to show a favorable performance on the expenses budget or vice versa.

OVERHEAD IN SERVICE DEPARTMENTS. Many departments are entirely overhead; for example, maintenance, plant protection, and superintendent's office. These are frequently called supporting or service departments because the cost of the manufacturing support departments, along with the overhead of the direct-labor departments, is properly chargeable as a manufacturing cost. In many companies, manufacturing overhead in general is called *burden*. Some companies treat service departments as revolving accounts; that is, they invoice the serviced departments. If this is done, the serviced departments must be budgeted for the costs of the servicing departments. In any event, the service departments themselves must be budgeted for purposes of planning and control. (Review chapter 8 for a discussion of the cost allocations necessary.)

CODING SYSTEM FOR BUDGETING. Because of the increased use of electronic data processing equipment, the various departments of a firm are usually designated by number. Thus:

Department	Number
Pattern department	01
Core room	02
Furnace room	03
Cleaning department	04
Machining	05
Assembly	06

Where there is more than one plant, with some duplication of departments by plant, the first digit can be used as a plant designator. Thus, assembly in the Des Moines plant, 16; assembly in the Dallas plant, 26.

Individual functions within each plant might be designated:

Supervision	001
Clerical labor	002
Supplies	114
Snow removal	279
Telephone	612

Thus, telephone costs in the assembly department at Des Moines would be 16–612; at Dallas, 26–612.

Such a numbering system permits management to determine not only individual *departmental* performances but also *functional* costs. Perhaps $100 expended on snow removal in each of ten departments is not a significant figure as a small item in a departmental budget of several thousand dollars, but $100 expended in each of twenty departments might result in an unacceptable total.

SCHEMATIC BUDGET FOR A MANUFACTURING DEPARTMENT. Figure 9.3 shows a schematic budget for a typical manufacturing department.

FOUNDRY DEPARTMENT—MAY
DES MOINES PLANT

Tons: 22		*Budgeted*
Direct Labor		1,600 hours
Materials		$2,200

Overhead

Account No.		
16-102*	Clerical labor	$475
16-103	Fuel	350
16-104	Heat and draw	900
16-105	Crane	600
16-106	Sand system	800
16-107	Tools and supplies	150
16-108	Repairs	100
16-501*	Supervision	1,000
16-502	Telephone	20
16-503	Depreciation	400

* Fixed and variable expenses can also be coded, in this illustration, by the third digit or in other systems by the use of additional digits.

Figure 9.3. Budget for a manufacturing department

SCHEMATIC BUDGET FOR A SUPPORTING DEPARTMENT. Figure 9.4 shows the budget for a supporting department. The difference between this budget and that presented in Figure 9.3 is that direct labor and materials are not usually factors in support departments.

MATERIAL TRANSFER DEPARTMENT—MAY
DES MOINES PLANT

Account No.		Budget
17-101	Supervision	$ 800
17-102	Clerical	500
17-103	Fuel	600
17-108	Repairs	900
17-126	Fork-lift drivers	2,200
17-503	Depreciation	1,300

Figure 9.4. Budget for a material transfer department

Nonmanufacturing Budget. In many industries sales costs are larger than manufacturing costs. Even where this is not true, it is just as important to plan and control the costs of selling the product, administration, and research and development as it is to plan and control manufacturing costs. Sales and administrative expenses are budgeted just like those of any other supporting department as illustrated in Figure 9.4 with different functional captions. Sales and administrative expenses are not distributed to the manufacturing departments but are written off against revenue in the accounting period in which they are incurred.

Research and development expenses present another aspect of the overhead problem. While they are budgeted in the same manner as a support department, their treatment may vary greatly on a firm's financial statements. Sometimes these expenses are capitalized and written off against the accounting periods that benefit from the products or processes developed. The problem presented by this view is simply that at the time a development decision may be necessary, we have no real way of knowing whether we have an electrostatic copier or an expensive toy on our hands.

Another treatment of research and development expenses is to distribute their cost among the operating departments. While this has the advantage of making those departments aware of the existence and necessity for the function, it has the drawback of charging managers for expenses over which they have no control and from which they usually can see no immediate benefit.

Still another method of treating research and development

expenses is to write them off against revenues in the period during which they were incurred, that is, to treat them exactly like sales and administrative overhead. The arguments for and against this practice are exactly the reverse of those for and against capitalizing research and development expenses.

FLEXIBLE BUDGET

If the budget is to be used as a valuable management tool, it must constantly be borne in mind that no matter how sophisticated the techniques may be, a totally accurate projection of what will occur is virtually impossible. It is necessary, therefore, to make plans that contemplate variations in the volume of business and production. While it is possible and even probable that changes in volume will affect the costs of direct labor and direct materials, the principal impact of changes in volume is on overhead budgets. Unless the budgets are changed because of changes in volume, control becomes impossible. For example, if production in a particular department is only 75 percent of that budgeted, the department is not necessarily being efficient in using only 90 percent of the budgeted supplies.

Capacity. In order to budget properly for both an ideal volume and variations from that ideal volume, it is first necessary to decide what is the budgetary norm. One school of thought holds that budgets should be built on the level that would result from maximum efficiency. Others hold that the setting of unattainable goals will soon vitiate any desire to try to do better.

THEORETICAL CAPACITY. The school of thought which believes that norms should be perfection would budget on the assumption that nothing ever goes wrong. It is interesting to note that the American steel industry consistently reported during World War II that it was working at more than 100 percent of capacity. The reason for this seeming anomaly was that normally scheduled maintenance, such as relining furnaces, was postponed wherever possible.

PRACTICAL CAPACITY. What the steel industry was reporting is referred to most frequently as *practical capacity*. This is the volume that can be attained if only the normal things go wrong;

that is, the plant will be closed only twice a year by blizzards, scrap will be normal, machine breakdowns will not be exceptional, and so on. Operations at practical capacity assume a volume of business that will allow for substantial order backlogs. One would assume that in time the possibility of attaining practical capacity would become relatively more difficult because of the addition of more plant capacity to take care of the backlog and because of the probability of competition.

NORMAL CAPACITY. *Normal capacity*, for a given budget period, is that volume of production which is expected during the period. A budget based on normal capacity is an expression of goals for the budgeted period in terms of efficiency and prices. Those who argue that budgeting should be in realistic rather than ideal terms point out that budgeting to normal capacity will pinpoint bottleneck departments and operations.

The major advantage of budgeting in terms of normal capacity is that realistic control figures are derived. Earlier reference was made to a situation where a department operated at 75 percent of budgeted capacity but used 90 percent of budgeted supplies. It is much simpler, for control purposes, to spot the exception of a plus or minus to a realistic figure than to adjust a theoretical figure to realistic terms and then interpolate the reported figures.

Fixed and Variable Overhead. Any book on cost accounting returns again and again to the problem of the two types of overhead, fixed and variable. There is a more complete discussion of this subject in earlier chapters, but some basic principles are given in this chapter.

FIXED OVERHEAD. *Fixed overhead* is overhead that, in a given accounting period, is predetermined and does not vary with the volume of production. However, this neat definition does not fit many situations. It has correctly been said that in the short run all overhead is fixed. For example, one usually thinks of power costs as an expense that varies directly with use. This is not true where there is a basic demand charge that must be paid whether power is used or not.

On the other hand, it is correctly said that in the long run all costs are variable. This is, in fact, the theory of using accelerated depreciation methods. Under the theory of accelerated depreciation, as the machine grows older it requires more and more maintenance. Taking more depreciation in the earlier years is an attempt to offset higher maintenance costs in later years so that, at least in theory, the *use* cost of the machine is the same from year to year. This practice could also be described as an attempt to weld two variable costs into one fixed cost.

VARIABLE OVERHEAD. *Variable overhead* is overhead that varies, in a given accounting period, with the volume of production. The simplest illustration of a purely variable cost would be commissions paid at a uniform rate to a sales representative who paid all his own expenses. Again, the definition does not really fit many situations. Under some conditions variable expenses are fixed; for example, wage costs of an employee entitled to a termination notice.

MIXED OVERHEAD. To say, in theory, that all overhead is really of a mixed nature does little good empirically. What, in fact, is it? One way to answer the question is to analyze the company's operating history. Another method, utilizing engineering techniques, is to analyze future costs based on the best knowledge currently available. Such a procedure is necessary when a new facility or the rearrangement of existing facilities is involved.

GRAPHIC ANALYSIS. It is interesting to plot actual overhead performance, item by item, against various bases. Contrary to expectations, one might find that an overhead item such as material-handling labor varies much more directly when compared with direct-labor hours than it does with tonnage of material handled. Graphic presentation in connection with major items is quite instructive.

Where there is some lag in the incurrence of overhead increments, for example, where another fork-lift truck driver is added only when twenty additional tons of materials per week must be moved, we might encounter the overhead pattern shown in Figure 9.5.

There will usually be a tendency for all overhead costs to follow the step pattern, but frequently the steps are too small to be important. A purely variable expense or one where the steps were inconsequential would graph as in Figure 9.6.

A demand charge for electric power with a lower charge when consumption had reached a given level, that is, graduated rates, would graph as in Figure 9.7.

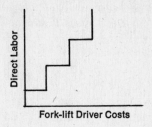

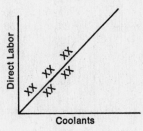

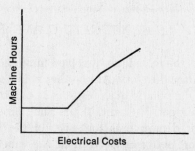

Figure 9.7. Typical variable overhead pattern

Many other methods to assist in distinguishing the fixed and variable elements are used. No method is precise, and a decision once reached will not be valid under changed operating conditions.

Schematic Flexible Budget. Figure 9.8 shows a schematic flexible budget built on the facts shown in Figure 9.3.

The budgets of supporting departments tend to vary in step patterns. For example, budgeted sales expenses, except for commissions, vary in relatively large amounts as programs or personnel are added or dropped.

FOUNDRY DEPARTMENT—MAY
DES MOINES PLANT

Tons produced		17.6	22	26.4	30.8
Direct-labor hours		1280	1600	1920	2240
Direct materials		$1760	$2200	$2640	$3080
Account No.					
16-102	Clerical labor	475	475	475	725
16-103	Fuel	315	350	385	410
16-104	Heat and draw	800	900	1000	1050
16-105	Crane	600	600	750	900
16-106	Sand system	600	800	900	1000
16-107	Tools and supplies	125	150	175	175
16-108	Repairs	100	100	125	125
16-501	Supervision	1000	1000	1000	1000
16-502	Telephone	20	20	20	20
16-503	Depreciation	400	400	400	400

Figure 9.8. Schematic flexible budget

HUMAN FACTORS IN BUDGETING AND REPORTING

Merely to discuss the techniques involved in budgeting is to omit a substantial part of the story. At no other point is the controller more in need of diplomatic qualities than in constructing and reporting on the budget. He must, at the same time, evaluate the requests of other departments for slices of the budget, report dispassionately on performance, and at the same time elicit a spirit of cooperation.

Constructing the Budget. It is only human to ask for more than one needs. If a manager thinks 100 hours are enough for a task and he obtains 125 in the budget, any performance under the latter figure makes him a hero. The man who asks for 90 and takes 95 can frequently expect less in the way of promotion than he who asks for 125 and takes 115 to do the same task. Accordingly, the controller (and the rest of the budget committee) is in an extremely delicate position. He must ask the various managers to set their own standards, evaluate those standards realistically, and convince all concerned that the slice of pie allotted to them is fair.

Profit Planning. Whatever the political or economic philosophy involved, planning for a profit in connection with a particular enterprise is a necessity. Assuming that the product of the enterprise is a social and economic good, a profit must be earned to provide an income on the capital invested, to replace the physical asset investment (depreciation allowances are rarely enough for this purpose), to provide a margin of safety for possible downturns in activity, and to attract capital for expansion.

At this earliest point in budgeting, a tempering of wisdom and foresight must overshadow mere numbers. The words "planning for a profit" are ambiguous. Do they mean for next month, for next year, for this division of the company only? It is easy to make next month look good by deferring regular maintenance until a future time. Next year can be made to look good at the expense of future years by discontinuing all research and development charged to revenues. Finally, a particular division or product can be favored by monopolizing funds available for sales promotion at the expense of other divisions or products.

Organization. No budget system, no matter how carefully constructed, will work unless it has the full support of the chief executive officer. Budgets take time to construct, and as has been mentioned, their mere construction can be more than a little abrasive. There is no point in conducting the exercise if the budget is to be ignored or unenforced.

If the firm has previously had no budget, the construction of the first budget can be an extremely useful tool in improving organization. In making a projection, it should become obvious who is in fact responsible for the particular activity; frequently, this is someone other than the organizational chart or title indicates. Both the budget and the organization should flow in identical channels. The organizational benefit of the budget is not limited to the first time a budget is constructed. Very often the force of circumstances will alter a previous organizational setup on a de facto basis. The asking of the same hard questions as each subsequent budget is constructed will help keep the theoretical facts pertaining to organization in line with the actual facts.

Reports. All the diplomatic skills expended in eliciting from the manager his forecasts as to his expected performance and in getting him to keep his forecasts realistic are nothing compared to the tact that must be used in reporting actual versus projected performance. Whether it is better to manage by the technique of unobtainable objectives or otherwise, it is still true that no one likes criticism. A coldly factual report stating who has not met the standards set without any attempt to find out why may very well build nothing but antipathy toward the whole process on the part of the operating people.

CONTROLLABLE AND NONCONTROLLABLE COSTS. Budgets should be constructed to include all costs to be incurred at a given level of management. Among these costs are those that are fixed and those that are variable as well as costs that are controllable by the particular manager and those that he cannot control. More recent thinking in the field suggests that a particular manager help plan and have reported to him only those costs that are controllable. The rationale is that the uncontrollable costs may be such a large part of the total as to foster an attitude of "What's the use?" on the part of the manager.

The terms *variable costs* and *controllable costs* are by no means synonymous. For example, unemployment taxes, FICA taxes, and workmen's compensation insurance are variable costs up to the point where they are no longer assessable (e.g., FICA taxes after wages reach prescribed limits). But they are most certainly not controllable by the manager.

On the other hand, at some level of management even a fixed cost can become controllable. Take the case of a marginal plant that has fixed costs of taxes, insurance, and depreciation. At the managerial level where a decision can be made to dispose of the plant, these costs are controllable.

A SCHEMATIC REPORT FORM. Figure 9.9 is a schematic report form explaining the known reasons for deviations at the Des Moines plant.

FOUNDRY DEPARTMENT—MAY
DES MOINES PLANT

	Budget	Actual	Difference*	Reason
Tons produced	22	20.5	1.5 U	Defective pattern design—scrap one day's production.
				Actual tonnage (before scrap, 21.3)
Direct-labor hours	1600	1622	22 U	Overtime—rework cores.
Direct materials	$2200	$2147	$ 53 F	Higher yield than average
Account No.				
16-102 Clerical labor	$475	$490	$ 15 U	Cost-of-living increase
16-103 Fuel	350	357	$ 7 U	
16-104 Heat and draw	900	879	21 F	
16-105 Crane	600	596	4 F	
16-106 Sand system	800	809	9 U	
16-107 Tools and supplies	125	150	25 U	
16-108 Repairs	100	190	90 U	Mould boxes damaged by failure to turn off vibrator
16-501 Supervision	1000	1000		
16-502 Telephone	20	28	8 U	Long-distance calls re damaged mould boxes
16-503 Depreciation	400	400		

* F-Favorable
U-Unfavorable

Figure 9.9. Schematic report form

CHAPTER 10

Standard Costs

For the year, the quarter, or the month, the budget will set the total direct materials or labor that the firm anticipates using over the period. This overall figure, however, has little meaning in terms of controlling day-by-day operations, setting prices for individual products, or making the necessary detailed entries in the books of account. Standard costs are used for all these purposes.

MANAGEMENT USES OF STANDARDS

It is possible to use standard costs in connection with the construction of a bridge, a building, or a ship, but the ordinary frame of reference is in terms of a batch of similar items of production. The words "items of production" are used rather than the word "product" because standards can be and are used in connection with subassemblies that may well be parts of several different products. For example, the same oil filters are used on most automobiles produced by the same manufacturer.

The standard is frequently expressed in terms of the individual item or component, but it is neither set nor reported on in that fashion. As a matter of fact, machine time for a particular operation might be expressed in seconds, but it would hardly be practical to keep track of actual time on each piece, even if each could be identified. It is the same with materials. In stamping parts from a strip of steel, one could hardly charge all the necessary scrap to the last piece; by the same token, one cannot ignore the cost of the materials consumed that do not wind up in the product.

The point of these two illustrations is that the labor and material standard is usually set and reported in terms of a batch, that is, 10 pieces, 100 pieces, and so on. Thus, the standard might be stated as $1 of materials for a particular item manufactured. The standard would be set, however, as $100 of materials for 100 pieces. Or, a standard might be stated as 45 seconds of machining time for each piece, which really means 75 minutes for 100 pieces.

Budgets and Standards. The overall departmental or company budget for labor and materials is really a compendium of the anticipated costs of all the individual batches for the budgetary period. In this sense, the words "standard" and "budget" are substantially interchangeable. The word "standard" is frequently used to define the minimum level of performance that is expected of employees before a bonus is earned. Where bonuses will be earned in varying amounts, the standard for payroll purposes and the standard for control purposes are not the same thing, and the use of the term to denote two different things is obviously confusing. Probably the best description of a standard for cost accounting purposes is the word "target."

Setting the Standard. Whenever a norm is set for performance, whether the area of involvement be overhead, sales, or direct costs, several questions keep recurring. Who should set standards, and what methods should be used? Should standards be set at ideal conditions, normal conditions, or at conditions that can be expected to prevail in the immediate future? The answers to these questions lie in the field of psychology rather than accounting and might well be different depending on the purpose to be served by using standard costs.

If the primary aim in using standard costs is to effect cost reductions, standards would probably be set at an ideal level, that happy but nonexistent condition where nothing ever goes wrong. The purpose here is to convey to the operating people that no matter how well they think they may have done, they could have done better. The psychologists must decide whether or not such standards may in time result in an attitude of hopelessness and accordingly become counterproductive.

If the essential consideration is control, standards would probably be set at reasonably attainable rates. Such standards should result in reasonably competitive prices, assuming the firm's equipment and production techniques are also reasonably competitive. Where reasonably attainable targets are used, a means exists to judge performances and to take corrective action when performance is substandard. Reasonable targets for performance are used by most firms and preferred by most writers on the subject.

Some firms use standard costs only for the purpose of making accounting entries easier. Where each batch is relatively small but there are a large number of batches, costs incurred in each batch most likely will differ, though probably not significantly. In times of rapid inflation, material costs tend to differ, almost between purchases, raising the obvious question whether standards should be the last price or the next price. Some firms, therefore, do not use standards as control devices but merely as a convenience for internal accounting so assemblies and subassemblies can receive uniform treatment as materials flow through the plant. Obviously, adjustments must be made in pricing work-in-process inventories for financial statement purposes, and standards used merely to facilitate intrafirm reporting should not be used for pricing or for financial statements.

There are several ways in which standards can be set. One method is to follow historic costs. Assuming that the historic costs can be updated for changes in prices and wage levels, this method has the virtue of simplicity. However, the setting of standards based on historic costs assumes that historic methods or performances are, in fact, optimum. A variant of this method is to set standards on the basis of discussions among those affected by standards: sales, production, and accounting. This variant does afford an opportunity for an exchange of ideas and suggestions, but it is subject to the same objection as historic costs. It is also subject to problems arising from personality differences.

Perhaps the best method of setting standards is to have the items and units of production studied by an industrial engineering department that would be independent of sales, production, and accounting. If products and methods are to be changed, such engineered standards are necessary. Where products do not change, such studies might well provide excellent opportunities for cost reduction. Even such an apparently insignificant change as a new kind of drill bit becoming available could well change the firm's method of drilling. The time necessary for drilling, the time necessary for tool dressing, and the setup time resulting from tool breakage might also be significantly changed.

Variances. "Management by exception" is a time-honored slogan that still works very well. If day-by-day management addresses itself immediately to those things that are off standard or that fail to meet the target, results of operations will tend to be optimal. In cost accounting, the difference between the standard cost and the actual cost is called a *variance*.

All variances are not necessarily bad. For example, the normal salable maple syrup from a gallon of raw materials might be three quarts. Assuming that three quarts is the standard, a yield higher than three quarts would be described as a favorable variance. A yield of less than three quarts would be called an unfavorable variance. In some process industries (chemicals, paper, and so on) the yield achieved for certain inputs is so important that it is checked on an hourly basis. This monitoring is done in terms of physical units, but the variances will also be reported in dollars.

If the standard cost system is used for purposes of control, prompt reporting and analysis of variances is essential. To report to a supervisor in the third week of September, when the financial statements for August have finally been balanced, reconciled, and disseminated, that during the first week of August there was an unfavorable variance of $100 on Batch 22 is simply not going to get anyone very excited about corrective action. Because of the necessity for prompt information for control purposes, many firms have abandoned the tie-in between their standard costs systems and their books of account. The difficulty here, of course, is that final reports, with all the detail accounted for, may tend to disagree with the aggregate of specific reports. It is impossible to generalize as to which is the better system for a specific firm at a specific time.

There is one point on which there is some agreement: Reports to operating managers should include only those costs and variances over which they have control. If total costs are reported for the sake of convenience, those costs and their variances that are not controllable at a given level of management should be so designated. The problem lies not in cost accounting but in supervisory morale.

MATERIALS STANDARDS

If the standard cost of materials for 1,000 units of Part X is $1,250, any difference between the $1,250 and the actual cost is a variance. The $1,250 should include scrap and a normal amount of spoilage, assuming attainable standards are used as the guide. It does not follow, however, that because the materials cost was $1,395 the departmental supervisor was guilty of substandard performance. For example, assume that the standard is based on an input of 5 tons of specialty steel at $250 per ton. Through no fault of the departmental supervisor, it became necessary to substitute more expensive materials costing $310 per ton. By a reduction of scrap, the supervisor has been able to produce the 1,000 units from only 4.5 tons of the more expensive steel. The result is two variances, one partially offsetting the other (Figures 10.1 and 10.2).

Price variance	$60 × 4.5 tons =	$270 U
Quantity variance	$250 × .5 ton =	125 F
Net ($1,395 − $1,250)		$145 U

U = Unfavorable
F = Favorable

Figure 10.1. Variances

It is frequently argued that the price variance shown above is incorrect as expressed—that it should be further subdivided to show what the price variance would have meant in terms of the standard quantity, 5 tons. That is:

Price variance	$60 × 5 tons =	$300 U
Joint or combined variance	$60 × .5 ton =	30 F
		$270 U

Figure 10.2. Price variance analysis

Which method should be used? If, considering the time required, the analysis of a particular variance results in useful and significant figures, it should probably be done. Too frequently, however, analysis in depth delays significant information needed for control purposes and proves nothing beyond the fact that the analyzer is adept at figures.

Price Variances. At what point should a variance from standard price be recorded? In theory, at least, the variance occurs when the materials are ordered, which causes the difference from our established norm. Basic accounting principles, however, bar us from making any entry in the books of account at this point and even from recognizing a purchase transaction in our published statements unless it is a large and unusual one.

Nevertheless, some firms would probably delay recognition of a price variance until the materials are actually requisitioned from stores. This is done simply as a matter of convenience, even though it is the poorest time if the purpose of the standard cost system is the prompt reporting of variances for control purposes. Assume that the more expensive material shown in Figure 10.1 was ordered specifically for the job. The entries would be as shown in Figure 10.3.

On purchase		
Stores (5 tons @ $310)	$1550	
Accounts payable		$1550
On requisition		
Work in process (4.5 tons @ $250)	1125	
Material price variance	270	
Stores		1395
On shipment		
(5 tons @ $250)		
Cost of sales materials	1250	
Work in process		1125
Material quantity variance		125

Figure 10.3. Price variance recognized when materials requisitioned

The production supervisor has been exonerated from blame in connection with this unfavorable variance. It does not follow that the purchasing department has failed in its responsibilities. Possibly the reason for the additional cost was that the sales department made a poor estimate of orders, and the purchasing department performed very well in finding acceptable materials at a "ballpark" price so that a rush order for a good customer could be filled.

Theoretically, at least, it is better to recognize price variances when the obligation for the materials is realized. This has the additional practical advantage of allowing all materials of the same kind that are present in the storeroom to be carried at the same price, which makes inventory-taking much easier. It is relatively simple to make any needed adjustments. The entries would appear as shown in Figure 10.4 for financial statement purposes.

On purchase		
Stores (5 tons @ $250)	1250	
Material price variance	300	
Accounts payable		1550
On requisition		
Work in process (5 tons @ $250)	1250	
Stores		1125
Material quantity variance		125
On shipment		
Cost of sales	1250	
Work in process		1250

Figure 10.4. Price variance recognized at purchase

There is a difference in the results that would appear on the financial statements, assuming that the half ton of more expensive material is on hand at the end of the accounting period. The net variance in Figure 10.3 is $145 (price variance of $270 less quantity variance of $125). In Figure 10.4 the difference is $175 (price variance of $300 less quantity variance of $125). The recognition of price variances at the time of invoice recording presupposes that substitute materials are worth no more than standard materials. Where the substitute materials are furnished from stores already on hand, this problem does not exist.

Volume Variances. The principal problem in connection with material quantity variances is their early recognition. Many firms take care of this simply by using forms readily distinguishable by size, shape, or color for requisitioning materials in excess of standard quantities. Similar distinguishing forms are used to record the return of materials denoting less than standard consumption. The accounting treatment for material quantity variances has already been illustrated in Figures 10.3 and 10.4.

As in the case of price variances, quantity variances may not be the fault of the production department. Substitute materials, failures in quality inspection upon the receipt of materials, rush orders, and a host of other problems may be the cause of quantity variances. Therefore, any attempt at control is only as effective as the investigation into the real reason for the variances.

LABOR STANDARDS

It is possibly more important for the industrial engineer to set standards for labor than for materials. A simple illustration will suffice. Most of us would go about painting a panel for a refrigerator or an automobile by keeping the panel stationary and moving the painting device. It is quite easy to visualize, however, that on a production-line basis it might involve much less handling and be cheaper to move the panel through a stationary painting device.

Labor Price Variances. Variances in the price of labor do occur, but they are more frequently the result of a union contract than the assignment of the wrong personnel to the task. Obviously, little control is gained by reporting such variances unless overtime is involved. The Fair Labor Standards Act calls for time and a half pay under certain conditions, and this is very frequently extended in union contracts. A glaring price differential of at least 50 percent in the cost of labor should not require the report of the cost accountant for its discovery. In short, this most important variance should be under control before it occurs rather than after it becomes a variance.

There are other areas where labor price variances can occur. If standards are adjusted only annually, a new union contract or a cost-of-living increase would automatically result in variances. If a base rate plus a bonus is used as the means of making payment, exceptionally high piecework performance or the low performance of an employee being broken in can result in substantial variances.

Labor Volume Variances. Where the number of hours to perform the task is other than the standard, a labor volume variance exactly parallel in concept to the materials volume variance is incurred. However, the question of how to handle setup time can be troublesome. *Setup time* is time spent either by the machine operator or a specialist in adjusting the machine so it can handle a different operation from the last one run on it. If the batches of work themselves are standard (e.g., if Operation 12 is never run unless 1,000 pieces are provided), it is probably simplest to include the setup time as part of the labor standard for Operation 12. However, where the size of the batches varies to some extent, it is probably better for control purposes to make setup time itself subject to a labor standard, separating it from the time required to run the production. It is frequently argued that setup time should be treated as part of factory overhead. This is reasonable unless it is a significant factor and easily identifiable with a particular production run.

Accounting for Labor Variances. Returning to the material variance illustration, the company is concerned with the variances in manufacturing 1,000 shaft housings. To simplify the illustration, assume that only one machining operation is performed on the shaft housings in this department but that each operation is to close tolerances and takes one-half hour. The rate for machinists is $3.50 per hour. The standards for the 1,000 units are 500 hours or $1,750. As authorized, workers worked 60 hours overtime but still only totaled 480 hours. General ledger treatment varies as to the time when the variances are to be recognized (Figure 10.5).

FINANCIAL STATEMENT TREATMENT OF LABOR AND MATERIAL VARIANCES

The question of how to handle the variances from standard in the direct costs of labor and materials is very similar to the question of how to handle over- or underabsorbed overhead. When a company has paid an excess price for materials as illustrated in

Work in process—Labor	1680	
(480 hours @ 3.50 std.)		
Labor price variance	105	
(60 hours @ 1.75 premium)		
Accrued payroll		1785
(420 hours @ 3.50)		
(60 hours @ 5.25)		
Cost of sales	1750	
(500 hours @ 3.50 std.)		
Work in process		1680
Labor volume variance		70
(20 hours @ 3.50 std.)		

or

Work in process at standard	1750	
Labor price variance	105	
Accrued payroll		1785
Labor volume variance		70
Cost of sales	1750	
Work in process		1750

Figure 10.5. Ledger entries: labor variances

Figure 10.1, has it added anything to the value of its finished product, assuming that some of the product remains in finished goods inventory at the end of the accounting period? In theory, this question is no different from asking if the company, by using less material than standard, has not created a value that financial statements for the period should recognize. Generally accepted accounting principles would indicate that the recognition of values proposed in the second question would be improper as an anticipation of profits before the product was sold. Granted that the anticipation of profits is objectionable; should not unfavorable variances be charged to the accounting period in which they were incurred or prorated over cost of goods sold and closing inventories?

Assume that the shaft housings discussed in this chapter sell for $7 each, that administrative and selling expenses are $2,000 for the accounting period, and that 750 units have been sold. There can be at least four different correct answers using the facts set forth in this chapter, depending on whether or not the net variances are prorated and on how material price variances are handled (Figures 10.6 through 10.9).

STANDARD COSTS: OVERHEAD

It is the usual practice to recognize and record labor and material variances in connection with the appropriate job order,

All variances charged to cost of sales

Sales (750 units @ $7)				$5,250
Cost of goods sold at standard				
Labor (½ hour @ $3.50)	1.75⎫			
Material (10 lb. @ .125)	1.25⎬ × 750		$2,250	
Add: Total variances				
Material: Per Figure 10.3.				
(270 — 125)			145	
Labor: Per Figure 10.5				
(105 — 70)			35	2,430
				$2,820
Selling and administrative expenses				2,000
Profit				$ 820

Figure 10.6. Material price variances recognized on requisition

All variances charged to cost of sales

Sales (750 units @ $7)				$5,250
Cost of goods sold at standard				
Labor (½ hour @ $3.50)	1.75⎫			
Material (10 lb. @ .125)	1.25⎬ × 750		$2,250	
Add: Total variances				
Material: Per Figure 10.4			175	
Labor: Per Figure 10.5			35	2,460
				$2,790
Selling and administrative expenses				2,000
Profit				$ 790

Figure 10.7. Material price variances recognized when purchase recorded

Sales		$5,250
Cost of sales at standard	$2,250	
Variances* $\dfrac{750}{1,000} \times \$180$	135	2,385
		$2,865
Selling and administrative expenses		2,000
Profit		$ 865

* Variances: Per Figure 10.6 $180

    750 Units sold/1,000 units manufactured.

*Figure 10.8. Material price variances recognized at
requisition. Variances prorated to cost of
sales and inventory*

Sales		$5,250.00
Cost of sales at standard	$2,250.00	
Variances* $\dfrac{750}{1,000} \times \$210$	157.50	2,407.50
		$2,842.50
Selling and administrative expenses		2,000.00
Profit		$ 842.50

* Variances: Per Figure 10.7 $210

    750 Units sold/1,000 manufactured.

*Figure 10.9. Material price variances recognized when
purchased. Variances prorated to cost of
sales and inventory*

batch, process order, or invoice for goods received. Overhead variances, on the other hand, can usually be recognized and recorded only on the basis of an elapsed time period, most frequently a month. It certainly does not follow that no action to control overhead can be taken until overhead expense is recorded and analyzed. Important dollar areas of possible variance should have immediate pragmatic controls. For example, a plant in which direct-labor volume may vary because of the availability of parts might well have departmental controls, effective automatically, on the ratio of hourly rated, indirect-labor employees to direct-labor employees.

The cost accountant's analysis of variances in overhead must ordinarily await the recording of expenses for the appropriate time period. Note that only analysis of variances is delayed; pragmatic controls are appropriate at all times. Furthermore, individual job orders may be priced at standard rates of overhead without awaiting end-of-the-month figures. This is the usual practice.

Fixed and Variable Overhead. The question of distinguishing fixed and variable overhead is a constant theme in cost accounting. Nowhere is it more vital than in a standard-cost system used for control that a proper distinction be made between fixed and variable overhead. Where the standard-cost system is used only for the purpose of accounting convenience, this distinction is not necessary; however, it may very well be necessary for the presentation of a financial statement.

To illustrate the necessity for the distinction between fixed and variable overhead, a rather simplistic example should suffice. Assume that our budget is incorrectly prepared as shown in Figure 10.10. The error, of course, is in classifying power costs

Fixed overhead		
Depreciation, etc.		$800
Power		$200
Total fixed overhead		$1,000
Variable overhead		500
Total overhead		$1,500
Units to be produced		100
Fixed overhead per unit	$1,000 ÷ 100	$ 10
Variable overhead per unit	$ 500 ÷ 100	$ 5

Figure 10.10. Necessity to distinguish between fixed and variable overhead

as fixed overhead when they are, in fact, variable.

Assume further that during the month under review, the following took place:

Fixed overhead		
Depreciation and the like		$800
Power		$150
Total fixed overhead		$950
Variable overhead		250
Total overhead		$1,200
Units produced		50
Fixed overhead per unit	$950 ÷ 50	$19
Variable overhead per unit	$250 ÷ 50	$ 5

The low volume of production is attributable to a strike in the plant of a manufacturer of a key component.

Using the erroneous classification of the power expense as fixed rather than variable overhead, the analysis would be:

Budgeted overhead	50 units × $15		$750
Actual overhead			1,200
Unfavorable			$450
Volume variance	50 units × $10		$500 U
Spending varianced budgeted		$1,000	
Actual		950	50 F
Net unfavorable variance			$450 U

However, had the power costs been classified properly as variable expenses, the budget would be:

Fixed overhead		$800
Variable overhead		700
Total overhead		$1,500
Units to be produced		100
Fixed overhead per unit	$800 ÷ 100	$ 8
Variable overhead per unit	$700 ÷ 100	$ 7

The total spending shown above would be the same but would be classified as follows:

Fixed overhead		$800
Variable overhead		400
Total overhead		$1,200

Units produced		50
Fixed overhead per unit	$800 ÷ 50	$16
Variable overhead per unit	$400 ÷ 50	$ 8

The analysis of the variances would be:

Volume variance	50 units × $8		$400 U
Spending variance			
Budgeted variable overhead	50 units × $7	$350	
Actual variable overhead		400	50 U
Net unfavorable variance			$450 U

Improper classification of a variable overhead item as fixed led to the incorrect analysis. While an analysis in and of itself may not prevent the overuse of power when production is less than planned, improper classification would result in the standard-cost system's becoming a hindrance to control, rather than a help.

Rate of Activity. Managers involved in the manufacturing activity cannot usually control the volume of production. Accordingly, unfavorable variances resulting from activity at lower levels than those budgeted are not usually considered controllable at the manufacturing level. Such variances may well be the measure of performance on the part of the sales department, possibly the purchasing department, and possibly the department in charge of scheduling. The point is that responsibility for all variances can be pinpointed.

If the foregoing statements are correct, it becomes just as necessary to be meticulous in the forecasts of production activity as it is to distinguish between fixed and variable overhead. In fact, the former may be more important. Unit overhead costs are the result of a simple fraction:

$$\frac{\text{Fixed costs}}{\text{Units produced}} + \frac{\text{variable costs}}{\text{units produced}} = \text{unit overhead costs}$$

The numerators and denominators are equally important.

It may well be true that prices are fixed in the long run by costs and in the short run by competition. For example, prices based on $800 in fixed costs spread over 100 units will in time vary from prices based on $800 in fixed costs spread over 50 units. In addition to the importance of the rate of activity for pricing, there are other reasons why so much care must be taken in estimating activity. As chapter 15 on capital budgeting points out, a decision to expand capital for a new machine tool might be appropriate for a volume of 100 units per month and inappropriate for a volume of 50 units per month.

Analysis of Overhead Variances. Variable overhead presents few problems in variance analysis because the analysis is essentially the same as for materials and labor. Fixed overhead, on the other hand, presents the problems of price and quantity complicated by considerations of the effect of the level of activity.

Some cost accountants argue that there should be no analysis at all of overhead variances beyond the reporting of spending variances. For example, if more is spent for a particular line item of overhead than has been budgeted, the reason for such expenditure is what should be investigated and reported. The rationale for this view is that whatever is gained by analysis of anything other than spending is not worth the time and effort.

Assume, for example, that the capacity of a plant at normal levels of activity is 100,000 hours of direct labor per month. If direct labor is currently at a level of 80,000 hours per month, it is certainly not necessary to wait for the analysis of fixed overhead variances to discover the reason for operating at less than capacity. The system of management controls, of which the standard-cost system is only one (albeit a most important one), should long since have told of a lack of orders, a breakdown of a critical machine, a failure to secure essential raw materials, and so on. In short, spending the time and money to analyze variances in fixed overhead probably adds little to control, and the analysis is not needed for purposes of financial accounting.

Nonetheless, three methods of overhead variance analysis and reporting are in use in industry and appear from time to time on the CPA examination. These three methods differ in the number of variances identified and analyzed; i.e., two, three, or four. Accordingly, the three methods will be examined using a common set of facts (Figure 10.11).

Budgeted

Fixed overhead	$5,000
Variable overhead	$10,000
Direct labor hours	5,000
Units produced	10,000
Fixed overhead per hour ($5,000/5,000 hours)	$1.00
Variable overhead per hour ($10,000/5,000 hours)	$2.00
Total overhead per hour	$3.00
Fixed overhead per unit ($5,000/10,000 units)	$0.50
Variable overhead per unit ($10,000/10,000 units)	$1.00
Total overhead per unit	$1.50

Actual Overhead

Fixed overhead	$4,950
Variable overhead	$9,900
Direct labor hours	4,500
Units produced	9,200
Fixed overhead per hour ($4,950/4,500 hours)	$1.10
Variable overhead per hour ($9,900/4,500 hours)	$2.20
Total overhead per hour	$3.30
Fixed overhead per unit ($4,950/9,200 units)	$ .538*
Variable overhead per unit ($9,900/9,200 units)	$1.076*
Total overhead per unit	$1.614*

* Figures rounded

Figure 10.11. Common facts for overhead analysis

TWO-VARIANCE METHOD. The two-variance method is used primarily for purposes of control. It has the dual advantages of simplicity and similarity to the methods used in reporting direct labor and direct material variances. These are important factors to consider when reports are made to managers who are not accountants. In the two-variance method, the purpose is to distinguish between those overhead expenses that are controllable at the plant level of management and those that are not. This is shown in Figure 10.12, using the facts set forth in Figure 10.11.

Stated another way, the underabsorbed overhead is $1,050, and the purpose of analysis is to separate this into its controllable and noncontrollable elements. Normal volume is 10,000 units (see

Overhead for units produced at standard rates
(9,200 units @ $1.50) $13,800

Actual overhead	
Fixed	$ 4,950
Variable	9,900
	$14,850
Less: Budgeted overhead	13,800
Total variance	$ 1,050 U

Figure 10.12. Two-variance method: total variance

Figure 10.11), but only 9,200 units were produced. Therefore, using the standard rate of overhead, $400 was not absorbed because of low volume (Figure 10.13).

Budgeted overhead at 9,200 unit capacity	
Fixed	$ 5,000
Variable (9,200 units @ $1.00)	9,200
	$14,200
Overhead for units produced at standard rates (see Figure 10.12)	13,800
Noncontrollable variance	$ 400 U

or

Normal production	10,000 units
Actual production	9,200 units
Underproduction	800 units
Fixed overhead per unit	× .50
Noncontrollable variance	$ 400 U

Figure 10.13. Two-variance method: noncontrollable variance

Obviously, $650 was controllable. This can also be computed in either of two ways as shown in Figure 10.14.

THREE-VARIANCE METHOD. In illustrating the two-variance method of analyzing overhead variances, we ignored the fact that it took only 4,500 hours to manufacture 9,200 units; whereas the standard at one-half hour per unit is 4,600 hours. The three-variance method analyzes the total variance in terms of the

Total actual overhead (see Figure 10.12)		$14,850
Budgeted overhead at 9,200 units		
(see Figure 10.13)		14,200
Controllable variance		$ 650 U

or

Actual variable overhead		$ 9,900
Budgeted variable overhead (9,200 units)		9,200
		$ 700 U
Less:		
Actual fixed overhead	$4,950	
Budgeted fixed overhead	5,000	50 F
Controllable variance		$ 650 U

Figure 10.14. Two-variance method: controllable variance

budget, efficiency, and level of activity or volume. Advocates of the two-variance method would point out that the efficiency in saving 100 hours has already been recognized in analyzing labor variances and that further analysis in connection with overhead is unnecessary.

Efficiency Variance. The efficiency variance is the difference between standard and actual hours for the goods produced, multiplied by the standard rate of overhead. In the situation used to illustrate the several methods, this is a favorable variance because 9,200 units were produced in 4,500 hours rather than the standard 4,600 hours (Figure 10.15).

Budgeted hours (4,600) × standard rate ($3.00)	$13,800
Actual hours (4,500) × standard rate ($3.00)	13,500
Efficiency variance	$ 300 F

Figure 10.15. Three-variance method: efficiency variance

Capacity. The capacity variance is the difference between hours worked and normal hours multiplied by the standard hourly fixed overhead rate. The capacity variance in the three-variance method is based on hours worked, whereas the controllable or volume variance in the two-variance method is based on units produced and is a function of over- or underabsorbed overhead (Figure 10.16).

Normal hours		5,000
Actual hours		4,500
		500
Fixed overhead rate	×	$1
Capacity variance		$ 500 U

or

Budgeted overhead @ 4,500 hours:	
Fixed	$5,000
Variable (4,500 hours @ $2.00)	9,000
	$14,000

Less:	
Actual hours (4,500 @ standard rate $3.00)	13,500
Capacity variance	$ 500 U

Figure 10.16. Three-variance method: capacity variance

Budgetary Variance. The budgetary variance is the difference between actual and budgeted overhead for the hours worked.

Actual overhead	$14,850
Budgeted overhead @ 4,500 hours	
(see Figure 10.16)	14,000
Budgetary variance	$ 850 U

Figure 10.17. Three-variance method: budgetary variance

The sum of the variances under the three-variance method is still the $1,050 unfavorable variance illustrated in Figure 10.12.

Efficiency variance	$ 300 F
Capacity variance	500 U
Budgetary variance	850 U
	$1,050 U

FOUR-VARIANCE METHOD. It was suggested earlier that the two-variance method of overhead analysis is incorrect because it fails to analyze variance arising from differences between standard hours and hours actually worked. The three-variance method is likewise criticized because it fails to analyze variances in spending. A four-variance method has been devised to correct these deficiencies. The four-variance method is a refinement of the two-variance method. Controllable costs are broken down into a spending variance and an efficiency variance, while the non-controllable variance is broken down into idle capacity and effectiveness variances.

Spending Variance. Except for the name, the spending variance under the four-variance method is exactly the same as the budgetary variance under the three-variance method (see Figure 10.17).

Efficiency Variance. The efficiency variance is the remainder of the controllable variance (see Figure 10.14). It is the difference between the overhead budget for the level of operations and the overhead budget for the units produced, a favorable variance in our illustration. Unfortunately, the nomenclature in general use is confusing because the efficiency variance under the three-variance method is not the same as that under the four-variance method. As a comparison of Figures 10.15 and 10.18 indicates, the three-variance method efficiency variance compares budgeted and actual hours at standard overhead rates; whereas the four-variance method efficiency variance compares the standard overhead for the actual level of operations with that for the number of units produced.

Budget for units produced			
Fixed overhead		$5,000	
Variable overhead (9,200 units @ $1.00)		9,200	$14,200
Budget for actual level of operations			
Fixed overhead		$5,000	
Variable overhead (4,500 hours @ $2.00)		9,000	14,000
Variance			$ 200 F

Figure 10.18. Four-variance method: efficiency variance

Idle Capacity Variance. The idle capacity variance is the difference between the hours actually worked and normal hours at the standard rate for fixed overhead. It is identical to the capacity variance under the three-variance method (see Figure 10.16).

Effectiveness Variance. The effectiveness variance is the difference between budgeted hours and the actual hours worked multiplied by the fixed overhead rate. It is also, of course, the difference between the controllable variance under the two-variance method and the idle capacity variance.

Standard hours for 9,200 units	4,600
Actual hours for 9,200 units	4,500
	100 F
Fixed overhead rate per hour	× $1
Effectiveness variance	$100 F

Figure 10.19. Four-variance method: effectiveness variance

Recapitulating the four variances, we find:

Spending	$ 850 U
Efficiency	200 F
Idle capacity	500 U
Effectiveness	100 F
	$1,050 U

Figure 10.20 presents a comparison of the three methods of analysis.

	Two		Four		Three
Noncontrollable:	$400 U	Idle capacity:	$500 U	Capacity:	$500 U
		Effectiveness:	100 F		
Controllable:	650 U	Spending:	850 U	Budget:	850 U
		Efficiency:	200 F	Efficiency:	300 F
	$1,050 U		$1,050 U		$1,050 U

Figure 10.20. Comparison of methods of overhead variance analysis

CHAPTER 11

Cost-Volume-Profit Analysis

Cost-volume-profit analysis is a valuable tool for measuring the efficiency of current operations. It is useful in the evaluation of pricing and selling decisions, planning for expansion or contraction of a business, and changing the cost structure of a business. Cost-volume-profit analysis is especially useful to businessmen because it ties together the entire planning process.

BREAK-EVEN ANALYSIS

The best way to begin the study of cost-volume-profit analysis is to examine a limited application called *break-even analysis*. Break-even analysis is the study of relationships between expenses, revenues, and volume (in terms of either units sold or dollars) to discover the point at which the firm can operate with neither profit nor loss.

Every businessman and accountant knows that costs react to a variety of factors and influences. It is axiomatic in accounting that wherever possible costs should be related to revenues. To assist in relating costs to revenues, costs are usually classified as *responsive* or *nonresponsive* to changes in revenues. Changes in costs are described, according to their response to revenues, as either *fixed* or *variable*. Fixed costs are nonresponsive, while variable costs are responsive to revenue changes. Some costs such as sales commissions or straight-line depreciation present little difficulty in classification. Sales commissions, for example, would be in direct proportion to revenues and are therefore variable in nature. Straight-line depreciation, on the other hand, would be completely independent of revenues and is an example of a fixed cost. Not all relationships are as clear-cut as these. For example, supervisory salaries in a factory may change with significant changes in output but not with minor changes. Some portion of these salaries is fixed, but there is also some variable portion. The allocation of the fixed and variable portions of each cost will be discussed later.

Assumptions and Limitations of Break-even Analysis. Break-even analysis can be a useful tool in determining the efficiency of operations for a firm at a given time. However, total reliance on this technique for all situations is not warranted. Some of the assumptions and limitations inherent in break-even analysis must be understood in order to make proper and rational use of this analytical tool.

For example, one assumption is that the relationship between costs and revenues can be represented by a straight line, at least within a limited range of observations. To the extent that (as is usually the case) the relationship is curvilinear or of some other form, break-even analysis is extremely limited.

Several other assumptions and limitations affect break-even analysis. The analyst assumes that such costs as heat, light and power, or indirect labor can be broken into fixed and variable components and that such components will retain their fixed or variable nature over the range being investigated. It is easy to see how a step-variable function does not fit such a definition. Another implicit assumption is that sales and production mixes remain constant. Obviously, if sales and/or production mixes change, the relationship between costs and revenues will change. Break-even analysis can be an important forecasting tool to aid in determining whether or not to undertake a planned change in production or sales mix. If unplanned changes occur, then any break-even analysis done previously will be worthless.

THE RELEVANT RANGE. The assumptions stated in the preceding section will not necessarily apply to any given situation under all possible developments. The best one can hope for is to find an area over which the assumptions will be relevant. The area for which the assumptions hold true is called the *relevant range*.

Whenever an assumption is made as to whether a cost is fixed or variable, such an assumption is valid only for the relevant range, and care must be taken to specify that range. An example of the application of this concept follows.

Assume that for every 100,000 widgets a factory produces per year, one factory supervisor paid $10,000 per year is required. Assume further that for the coming year the anticipated level of production of widgets will be somewhere between 810,000 and 870,000 units. This means that for a production range of 810,000 to 870,000 units the cost will be fixed at $90,000 per year for supervisory salaries (nine supervisors at $10,000 each). However, if production were reduced to only 750,000 units, which is outside the relevant range, the fixed-cost determination would no longer be valid.

Graphic Approach to Break-even Analysis. The principles and techniques involved in break-even analysis can be illustrated by applying them in a simple case, using first a graphic analysis and then, in the next section, a mathematical analysis.

BASIC EXAMPLE. George Town plans to open a factory to produce a new type of ventilating device. The devices will sell for $300 each, and the variable costs of production are expected to be $150 per unit. The fixed costs of operating the factory are expected to be about $120,000. How many units must be sold to break even?

CONVENTIONAL BREAK-EVEN CHART. The conventional break-even chart (Figure 11.1) would be prepared as follows to depict the problem graphically:

1. Prepare the first quadrant of an area graph with the origin (intersection of x and y axes) labeled zero.

2. Label the x axis (horizontal line) as units of output.

3. Label the y axis (vertical line) as dollars. (This will represent both costs and revenues.)

4. Plot the sales line starting at the zero point, and extend it to the limit of the chart.

5. Plot the fixed costs parallel to the x axis (units of output).

6. Plot the variable costs starting at the intersection of the fixed costs and the y axis (at $120,000 in the example). This variable costs line becomes the total costs line as well.

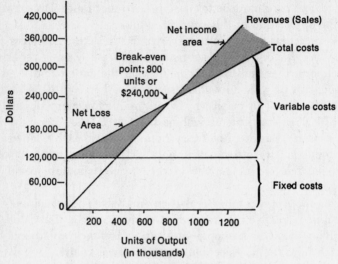

Figure 11.1 Conventional break-even chart

The break-even point, which is at the point of intersection of the total costs line and the revenues line, is 800 units, or $240,000. Should sales fall below 800 units, losses will be incurred; should sales rise above 800 units, profits will accrue to the business. Thus, the amount of profit or loss can be read from the chart by measuring the distance between the revenues line and the total costs line at any given output.

A PREFERRED BREAK-EVEN CHART. Many accountants prefer a modified form of the break-even chart. The difference between the two charts (conventional and modified) comes entirely from the order in which costs are plotted. On the conventional chart, fixed costs are graphed first, and variable costs will not intersect with the origin unless fixed costs are zero. This can be seen in Figure 11.1 where the variable costs line (total costs line) intersects the vertical axis at $120,000. The preferred break-even chart will have the variable costs line intersect at the origin as in Figure 11.2. The second chart is usually preferred because it illustrates at a glance the direct contribution of each dollar of sales over and above the variable cost of obtaining those sales.

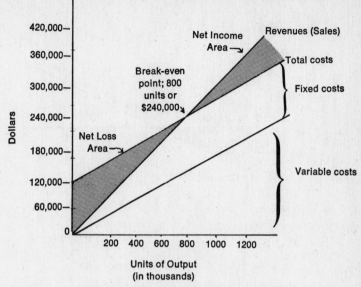

Figure 11.2. Preferred break-even chart

With the conventional chart, confusion sometimes arises over this very significant detail, particularly where operations are below the break-even point.

PROFIT GRAPH. Still another technique for graphing break-even analysis is the use of the *profit graph* or *profit-volume chart*. This chart does not give the detail of the break-even chart, but it does express the dollar profit or loss in terms of dollar sales. The facts in the basic example are illustrated in Figure 11.3.

From the graph, it can be seen that if sales are $0, loss is $120,000; if sales are $480,000, profits are $120,000. It can also be determined that the break-even point is $240,000 in sales.

Mathematical Approach to Break-even Analysis. In addition to the graphic or chart approach illustrated, there are also mathematical techniques that can be employed to assist in break-even analysis. While the graphic method is easy to explain and useful for demonstration to others, it is time-consuming to draft accurate charts. Inasmuch as the break-even point is a function of the relationship among fixed costs, variable costs, sales revenue, and volume, and this relationship can be expressed mathematically, it

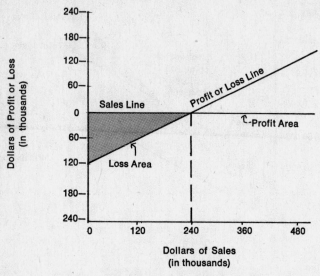

Figure 11.3. *Profit graph*

will ordinarily be faster and easier to determine the break-even point by the use of the following (conventional) formula:

$$\text{Break-even point} = \frac{\text{total fixed costs}^*}{1 - \dfrac{\text{variable costs}}{\text{sales}}}$$

* A better way of expressing this equation is:

$$\text{Break-even point} = \frac{\text{total fixed expenses}}{\dfrac{\text{contribution margin}}{\text{sales}}}$$

Using the same basic fact situation,

$$\text{Break-even point} = \frac{\text{total fixed costs } (F)}{1 - \dfrac{\text{variable costs } (V)}{\text{sales } (S)}} = \frac{\$120,000}{1 - \dfrac{150}{300}} = \$240,000$$

The break-even point can be expressed in terms of units by dividing sales ($240,000) by the selling price per unit ($300), which would yield 800 units. The number of units required to break even could also be directly calculated by:

$$\frac{\text{Fixed costs}}{\text{Sales price/unit—Variable cost/unit}} = \frac{\$120,000}{300 - 150} = 800 \text{ units}$$

THE PROFIT FUNCTION

So far, the discussion of cost-volume-profit analysis has centered on the break-even point. All businesses, however, want to do something better than just break even. Cost-volume-profit analysis is incorporated into break-even analysis by adopting a profit function. In this case the formula would read:

$$\begin{array}{l}\text{Sales necessary to reach} \\ \text{desired profit}\end{array} = \frac{\text{fixed costs } (F) + \text{desired profit } (P)}{1 - \dfrac{\text{variable costs } (V)}{\text{sales } (S)}}$$

To illustrate, using the facts of the basic example plus the additional fact that George Town wanted to make a $30,000 profit, the formula to find the level of sales necessary to achieve the profit goal would be stated as follows:

$$\frac{F + P}{1 - \dfrac{V}{S}} = \frac{120,000 + 30,000}{1 - \dfrac{150}{300}} = 300,000$$

This technique is also useful to determine the impact on profits of a change in selling prices, fixed costs, variable costs, or volume.

Impact of Increase in Selling Prices. Assume that selling prices rise to $375 and all other factors in the basic example remain the same. The break-even point would fall to $200,000 as shown below:

$$\frac{F}{1 - \dfrac{V}{S}} = \frac{\$120,000}{1 - \dfrac{150}{375}} = \$200,000$$

If the profit goal remained at $30,000, then the sales required to reach that point would fall to $250,000; thus,

$$\frac{F + P}{1 - \dfrac{V}{S}} = \frac{\$120,000 + \$30,000}{1 - \dfrac{150}{375}} = \$250,000$$

Impact of Change in Variable Costs. Return to the facts of the basic example but assume that variable costs change from $150 per unit to $200 per unit. Applying the formula, we see that the break-even point would rise from $240,000 to $360,000.

$$\text{Break-even point} = \frac{F}{1 - \frac{V}{S}} = \frac{\$120,000}{1 - \frac{200}{300}} = \$360,000$$

Contribution Margin. Another term for that part of the equation for break-even analysis represented by

$$1 - \frac{\text{Variable Costs per Unit}}{\text{Sales Price per Unit}}$$

is the *contribution margin ratio* or *contribution income ratio*. The contribution margin is the excess of sales over variable costs and is the margin available to cover fixed costs and profit. As this ratio increases, the firm is better able to recover fixed costs and generate profits. This ability to generate profits is frequently referred to as the firm's *margin of safety*. The margin of safety is simply the amount by which sales may fall before a loss is incurred.

The concept of marginal costs and revenues and contribution margin is further explored in chapter 13, which deals with direct costing.

CHAPTER 12

Sales and Production Mix

Analysis of sales and production mix can be a most rewarding exercise in business management if the analysis is limited to planning with an "if-we-change-this, profits-will-change-by-that" type of approach. This analysis is also useful in isolating the impact of such changes on current profits. Sales-mix analysis and production-mix analysis are merely measures of deviations from some desired norm in order to predict the impact on profits of some change in the order of doing things. Sales- and production-mix analyses are extensions of variance analysis as discussed in chapter 10. In this chapter, sales and production mix are isolated from quantity and price variances, although practically, such isolation would be unrealistic.

IMPACT OF CHANGES IN SALES MIX

The sales mix is the proportion that the total sales of each product bears to the total sales of all products of the firm.

In Figure 12.1, the budgeted sales, variable costs, and contribution margins of the Skider Corporation are presented for the current year. This budget is based on a planned sales mix of 100,000 widgets and 50,000 nidgets for a total output of 150,000 units.

Figure 12.2 shows what actually happened during the current year. Notice that sales prices and contribution margin have changed. In this particular case, variable costs have been kept constant because changes in variable costs will be discussed later.

A comparison of Figure 12.2 with Figure 12.1 shows that the Skider Corporation, for the current year, actually earned $324,000

SKIDER CORPORATION

BUDGETED SALES
CURRENT YEAR

	Units	Unit Price	Sales	Unit Variable Costs	Total Variable Costs	Contribution Margin	Percent*
Widgets	100,000	$3.00	$300,000	$2.40	$240,000	$ 60,000	20
Nidgets	50,000	6.00	300,000	4.20	210,000	90,000	30
Totals	150,000	$4.00†	$600,000	$3.00†	$450,000	$150,000	25

* Contribution margin percent is computed by dividing the contribution margin by sales.
† The total unit price and total unit variable cost shown are obtained by computing the weighted-average selling price and weighted-average variable cost. This is done by dividing total sales and total variable costs by total units.

Figure 12.1

SKIDER CORPORATION

ACTUAL RESULTS
CURRENT YEAR

	Units	Unit Price	Sales	Unit Variable Costs	Total Variable Costs	Contribution Margin	Percent
Widgets	90,000	$3.20	$288,000	$2.40	$216,000	$ 72,000	25
Nidgets	90,000	7.00	630,000	4.20	378,000	252,000	40
Totals	180,000	$5.10	$918,000	$3.30	$594,000	$324,000	35.3

Figure 12.2

in contribution margin as opposed to the budgeted $150,000. The factors that contributed to this increase in profitability will be discussed in the next sections. The best way to do this is to break down the impact of changes in the sales mix and in the contribution margin; first, by isolating the change in sales mix; second, by isolating the change in sales prices. If there has been a change in costs, those changes will also have to be separated. The first step in preparing the calculation of the different variances would be to compare the actual percentages of production with those budgeted.

	Budgeted	Actual
Widgets	⅔	½
Nidgets	⅓	½

Change in Sales Mix Quantified. The mix variance for each product is defined as follows:

Mix variance = [(Budgeted mix ratio × Actual total unit quantity) − Actual product quantity] × Budgeted contribution margin

Therefore:

Mix variance
  for widgets = [(⅔ × 180,000) − 90,000] × $.60 = $18,000 U
Mix variance
  for nidgets = [(⅓ × 180,000) − 90,000] × $1.80 = $54,000 F

Total mix variance $36,000 F

U = unfavorable
F = favorable

Change in Quantities Sold Quantified. The quantity variance for each product is defined as follows:

Quantity variance = [(Budgeted mix ratio × Actual total unit quantity) − Budgeted product quantity] × Budgeted contribution margin

Therefore:

Quantity variance
  for widgets   = [(⅔ × 180,000) − 100,000] × $.60 = $12,000 F
Quantity variance
  for nidgets   = [(⅓ × 180,000) − 50,000] × $1.80 = $18,000 F

Total quantity variance $30,000 F

Change in Sales Price Quantified. The sales price variance for each product is defined as follows:

Sales price variance = (Actual unit price —
                                       Budgeted unit price) × Actual sales units

Therefore:

Sales price variance
  for widgets   = ($3.20 — $3.00) × 90,000 = $18,000 F
Sales price variance
  for nidgets   = ($7.00 — $6.00) × 90,000 = $90,000 F

Total sales price variance $108,000 F

Recapitulation. Summarizing these calculations yields:

	Widgets	Nidgets	Total
Mix variance	$18,000 U	$54,000 F	$36,000 F
Quantity variance	12,000 F	18,000 F	30,000 F
Sales price variance	18,000 F	90,000 F	108,000 F
Total variance accounted for	$12,000 F	$162,000 F	$174,000 F

Had there been a variance arising from changes in variable costs, this variance would be handled in the same way as the change in the selling price. In other words, if A = the actual unit cost, B = the budgeted unit cost, and S = the actual sales in units, then $(A—B) \times S$ = the variable cost variance.

CHANGES IN MATERIAL MIX

Many products can be manufactured in several different ways. For example, the manufacturer can use more of an inferior quality material to substitute for a more expensive material and still have the same quality of finished product with more waste. Where this is possible a computation is necessary to determine whether it is better to use combination A or combination B. This computation is similar to that used for the analysis of sales mix variance:

SKIDER CORPORATION
STANDARDS FOR WIDGET PRODUCTION*

120 pounds of B @ $1.10 = $132.00
60 pounds of S @ $2.00 = 120.00
20 pounds of T @ $7.00 = 140.00

Total cost $392.00 for 200 pounds of standard mix

* The standard mix of 200 pounds will normally yield 196 finished widgets at a
standard cost of $2.00 per widget ($392 cost of materials ÷ 196 finished units).

Figure 12.3 shows the results of operations for the current year
for the Skider Corporation.

SKIDER CORPORATION
ACTUAL USE OF RAW MATERIALS

86,000 pounds of B @ $1.01   = $ 86,860
31,000 pounds of S @ $2.10   =   65,100
15,000 pounds of T @ $7.30   =   109,500

132,000

            Total cost $261,460
Good output: 124,460 widgets at
    a standard cost of $2.00 per unit =   248,920

Total unfavorable material variance
    to explain $ 12,540

Explained as follows:
Mix variance $ 2,880 U
Quantity or yield variance   9,800 U
Price variance   140 F

    Total variance explained $12,540 U

Figure 12.3

In the following calculations of variance it is assumed that
there are no raw-material inventories and that purchases are
made as needed. Therefore, all price variances relate to production. If there were inventories of raw materials, the raw materials would be released to production at standard cost, and the
variance would be recognized at the time of receipt rather than
when the goods are put into production.

Calculation of Mix Variance. The mix variance is computed as follows:

$$\text{Mix variance} = [(\text{Budgeted mix percentage} \times \text{Actual total quantity}) - \text{Actual product quantity}] \times \text{Standard cost}$$

$$
\begin{aligned}
B &= [(.60 \times 132,000) - 86,000] \times \$1.10 = \$\ 7,480\ \text{U} \\
S &= [(.30 \times 132,000) - 31,000] \times \$2.00 = \$17,200\ \text{F} \\
T &= [(.10 \times 132,000) - 15,000] \times \$7.00 = \$12,600\ \text{U} \\
&\qquad \text{Total} \qquad\qquad\qquad\qquad\qquad\qquad\ \ \$\ 2,880\ \text{U}
\end{aligned}
$$

Calculation of Quantity or Yield Variance. In calculating the yield variance it is necessary to relate the finished product output to the standards set by the company. In the illustrated case, the final output at standard has a ratio of .98 to the input (.98 widgets per pound of input or $\dfrac{196\ \text{widgets}}{200\ \text{pounds}}$). Thus, the standard usage of materials for 124,460 pieces is 127,000 pounds$\left(\dfrac{124,460}{.98}\right)$. Five thousand pounds of material in excess of standard have been used.

Using this data in the equation for determining yield variance:

$$\text{Yield variance} = [(\text{Budgeted mix percentage} \times \text{Actual total quantity}) - \text{Budgeted product quantity}] \times \text{Standard cost}$$

$$
\begin{aligned}
B &= [(.60 \times 132,000) - 76,200] \times \$1.10 = \$\ 3,300\ \text{U} \\
S &= [(.30 \times 132,000) - 38,100] \times \$2.00 = \$\ 3,000\ \text{U} \\
T &= [(.10 \times 132,000) - 12,700] \times \$7.00 = \$\ 3,500\ \text{U} \\
&\qquad \text{Total} \qquad\qquad\qquad\qquad\qquad\qquad\ \ \$\ 9,800\ \text{U}
\end{aligned}
$$

Calculation of Price Variance. The price variance is the last of three variances which must be computed for a thorough analysis of the causes of deviations from the budget of the Skider Corporation. The price variance is merely:

$$\text{Price variance} = (\text{Actual unit cost} - \text{Budgeted unit cost}) \times \text{Actual product quantity}$$

$$
\begin{aligned}
B &= (\$1.01 - \$1.10) \times 86,000 = \$7,740\ \text{F} \\
S &= (\$2.10 - \$2.00) \times 31,000 = \ \ 3,100\ \text{U} \\
T &= (\$7.30 - \$7.00) \times 15,000 = \ \ 4,500\ \text{U} \\
&\qquad \text{Total} \qquad\qquad\qquad\qquad\quad\ \ \$\ \ 140\ \text{F}
\end{aligned}
$$

Analysis of Changes in Material Mix and Yield. From the information presented above it can be seen that the Skider Corporation suffered higher costs and a less efficient output or yield because of a change in input. The mix variance led to higher costs of $2,880, and the lower yield cost the company $9,800. The company should investigate whether these excess costs are caused by the use of lower grade materials or by some foul-up in production.

CHANGES IN DIRECT LABOR AND VARIABLE OVERHEAD

These topics were covered fully in chapter 10 on standard costing. The four-variance method should be given particular attention.

CHAPTER 13

Direct Costing

With changes in products and markets, and more sophisticated methods of production, cost accountants have had to improve their techniques. In addition to the standard costing and flexible budgeting techniques discussed in other chapters, there is a more recently developed reporting method that management has found extremely useful, *direct costing.**

Direct costing is an attempt to resolve the perennial problem of allocating fixed expenses to appropriate products and time periods. Direct costing departs from other approaches in maintaining that fixed costs are sunk costs and are really not applicable to the going concern, that is, the firm that intends to stay in business. The proponents of direct costing claim that fixed costs are not meaningful in terms of the product manufactured in a given accounting period. All other cost allocation methods allocate fixed costs in some manner into unit product costs and show such allocation in both opening and closing inventory values.

DEVELOPMENT OF DIRECT COSTING

Direct costing did not suddenly arrive on the industrial scene as a fully developed concept. There was a period during which various techniques were devised, applied, and modified in an attempt to supply the information needed by management for the efficient conduct of the business.

* Direct costing is also called marginal costing or variable costing in other textbooks.

Full-Absorption Costing. Until the beginning of the twentieth century, all manufacturing costs were charged to the product produced during the accounting period the costs were incurred or accrued. This procedure of accounting for all manufacturing costs is known as *full-absorption costing*. Given an accounting period sufficiently long, that is, several years, the distortions caused by absorption costing would not be too misleading. However, when reporting periods are monthly or even annual, product costs, determined by the method of charging all costs when incurred or accrued, can result in radical variations in unit costs simply because of changes in the volume of production. These variations occur in unit costs even though sales remain at a constant level, for example:

	May	June	July
Production	3,000 units	2,000 units	1,000 units
Variable labor	$3,000	$2,000	$1,000
Variable materials	1,500	1,000	500
Fixed costs	1,500	1,500	1,500
Unit cost	$ 2.00	$ 2.25	$ 3.00

It was recognized that the foregoing was unsatisfactory because, in all cases in this example, variable labor and material costs together were the same, $1.50 per unit. Fixed costs varied, depending on production, from $.50 to $.75 per unit to $1.50 per unit, changing the total unit cost from $2.00 to $3.00.

Predetermined Overhead Rates. It became obvious to accountants and managers that pricing and other management decisions could not very well be predicated on the month-to-month fluctuation in fixed unit costs caused merely by changes in production. Accordingly, the concept of *predetermined overhead rates* came into vogue. A variety of rate-setting methods was used for such predetermination. Some firms used ideal rates; others, normal rates; and still others, average annual rates. Under the concept of predetermined overhead rates, fixed costs were charged to cost of sales as part of product cost at a predetermined rate, the balance of actual overhead carried on interim financial statements as either an asset or as a reduction of assets depending on whether overhead was under- or overabsorbed. When the volume of production varied substantially from one interim period to another, the disposition of the over- or underabsorbed overhead account was obviously very difficult and, more often than not, resulted in substantial distortion of reported profits on interim financial statements. When the volume of production does not fluctuate materially from month to month, predetermined overhead rates will work fairly well. They are widely used today.

Flexible Budgeting. The next concept to evolve was that of *flexible budgeting*, in which fixed costs are budgeted at anticipated (rather than normal or ideal) rates of production. Where the volume of production does fluctuate, flexible budgets must be reviewed periodically and regularly.

Perhaps the chief difficulty with flexible budgeting arises when there is a substantial difference in volume between production and sales in a given month, and it is anticipated that the volume of both production and sales will fluctuate markedly during the year. Distortions in profit reporting are inevitable in such circumstances. Furthermore, because fixed costs are applied to unit costs, there will tend to be variation in unit cost depending on the month of manufacture. Flexible budgeting is discussed in more detail in another chapter.

DIRECT COSTS. The terms *direct costing, marginal costing*, and *variable costing* are used interchangeably to describe a management tool that has evolved since World War II. Unfortunately, the words "direct costs," "marginal costs," and "variable costs" are used in other traditional cost accounting concepts. Direct costs are frequently used to describe those labor and material costs that are expended directly on the product. Marginal costs are used to mean incremental costs. Variable costs are often used in the context of nondirect costs, which are a function of the volume of production. In this chapter, direct costs are those costs that vary with the volume of production; it is immaterial whether they are labor, material, or overhead.

FIXED COSTS. Direct costs are distinguished from those that do not vary with the volume of production. For the purposes of this chapter, nondirect costs are termed *fixed* or *period costs*. It is generally recognized that costs can be classified into four groups:

1. Totally variable costs, e.g., costs of materials contained in the end product.

2. Semivariable costs, e.g., power costs. There is usually a minimum fixed cost even when there is no consumption; thereafter, costs are frequently graduated depending on the volume of consumption.

3. Semifixed costs, e.g., supervisory salaries. These are essentially the same as semivariable costs, but the fixed elements predominate. Most writers agree that there is no real distinction between semivariable and semifixed costs.

4. Fixed costs, e.g., property taxes based on the valuation of real estate or machinery. Such costs are fixed because their base is ad valorem, and their incidence is the same in a given year, whether volume is zero or maximum capacity.

It should be obvious that the distinction between variable and fixed costs is frequently a matter of expediency. Mere catchword definitions will not work. For example, depreciation charges based on anticipated useful life are usually fixed costs, whereas depreciation charges based on units of production are usually variable. Moreover, certain costs that are usually thought of as direct and variable are in fact fixed. For example, where machine operators are salaried or covered by a guaranteed, annual-wage union contract, this seeming direct and variable cost is fixed in reality and must be treated as if it were overhead.

The Concept of Direct Costing. As we have seen, absorption costing and flexible budgeting costing may result in substantial differences in unit cost, depending on the volume of manufacturing activity. Direct costing was conceived to separate costs directly related to the product from all other costs. Those costs related to the product will vary in total according to changes in volume of production, but unit costs and gross profit per unit will tend to remain the same in all accounting periods.

Costs Included in Direct Costing. Direct costs can include labor, materials, and overhead; the basic criterion is whether or not they vary with the volume of production. All other costs are treated as period costs; that is, they are a function of time. Another way of stating the theory of direct costing is that the application of fixed costs to units of production is so difficult, time-consuming, and arbitrary that one should not attempt to do so.

USE OF DIRECT COSTS WITH A STANDARD-COST SYSTEM. In a direct-costing system, direct costs are handled in exactly the same manner as in an absorption cost system. There is nothing in a direct-costing system that is in any way incompatible with a standard-cost system; variance from a predetermined norm of either direct costs or fixed costs can be evaluated and reported in exactly the same way under either system.

EXAMPLE OF STATEMENT PRESENTATION: DIRECT COSTING. Below is an example of statement presentation in a direct-costing system.

	Actual	Budgeted
Sales	$100,000	$100,000
Less: Variable cost of sales	60,000	62,000
Marginal income (contribution margin)	40,000	38,000
Less period costs:		
Manufacturing	20,000	19,000
Administrative	7,000	7,000
Selling	3,000	3,000
Total period costs	30,000	29,000
Profit before taxes	$ 10,000	$ 9,000

The first subtotal is entitled marginal income rather than gross profit. The statement is expandable to meet the needs and desires of the user.

Advantages of Direct Costing. 1. Operating information applicable to supervisory personnel is more readily gathered and is disseminated more easily and rapidly. 2. Operating management is generally not sophisticated in the volume/cost relationship. Reporting total cost is both confusing and counterproductive. 3. Marginal income per unit remains constant, making it easier to comprehend and measure the effects of volume. Marginal income is sometimes called the "contribution margin," i.e., the contribution to meeting period costs and/or to making a profit.

4. When more than one product is involved, direct costing is particularly beneficial. The allocation of direct period costs between products must be arbitrary at least in part. By measuring only the marginal income (contribution margin) of each product, its impact on the profitability of the firm is more readily discernible. Furthermore, such an analysis might very well assist in the allocation of resources between products. 5. The same rationale of analysis is appropriate between sales offices or territories and between plants.

Disadvantages of Direct Costing. 1. Direct costing tends to exaggerate swings in the business cycle. This is particularly true where production has seasonal cycles. 2. The present trend toward automation and some sort of guaranteed annual income for production workers means that an increasingly larger portion of costs is definable as period costs. This claim is frequently met by the argument that the trend itself makes it even more important to clarify the impact of these more or less fixed costs on the profit/volume relationship. 3. While the National Association of Accountants recommends direct costing as a viable management tool, financial statements based on direct costing are unacceptable to the Internal Revenue Service, the Securities and Exchange Commission, the American Institute of Certified Public Accountants, and the American Accounting Association. This opposition is based on the single fact that no provision is made for fixed costs as a part of opening or closing inventories.

DIFFERENCES IN REPORTING BETWEEN DIRECT AND ABSORPTION COSTING

The difference in reporting between direct- and absorption-cost systems is in operating statement presentation. Figure 13.1 illustrates the difference in the absorption of fixed overhead into closing inventories, plus or minus the resulting differences in opening inventories of the subsequent period. Obviously, it is a relatively simple matter to reconcile the two statements, and the fact that a direct-costing system can be used only internally is not a good reason against adopting it.

THE CONTRIBUTION MARGIN

An additional advantage of the direct-costing concept is found in situations where institutional costs are difficult, if not impossible, to allocate among the various divisions, plants, departments, or products with which they are in some degree connected. For example, assume a labor relations staff at company headquarters. A distribution of costs among twenty plants based on the proportionate number of employees at each plant is mathematically simple and has the virtue of precision. As a practical matter, however, such an allocation may have little, if any, relation to the actual expenditure of time and effort at each individual plant.

The contribution margin approach is really very simple. It calls for the allocation of only those costs that are specifically identifiable with a particular division, plant, department, or product. All other costs are deemed to be costs of the firm, and the net revenues of the various segments of the firm contribute to the payment of those costs and to the firm's overall profits. Fixed costs of the several segments being analyzed are also separated, so that decisions can be made more rationally as to their long- and short-run effects.

Figure 13.2 illustrates the contribution margin approach as applied to the two plants of a firm. Figure 13.3 subdivides Plant X by products, using the same concepts as between plants. The contribution margin is separated from the short-term margin because it is most sensitive to changes in volume as illustrated in chapter 11. The short-term margin is distinguished from the long-term margin because decisions as to pricing and asset utilization must frequently be made without reference to sunk costs.

The short-term margin in Figure 13.3 is greater than that in Figure 13.2 because the controllable and identifiable fixed costs are greater for Plant X in Figure 13.2 than for Plant X in Figure 13.3. Sales promotion expenses, for example, might be easily identifiable with a division or a plant, but not with products of that plant. The noncontrollable and identifiable fixed costs differ between the two figures for the same reason.

OCTOBER

	Direct Costing		Absorption Costing	
Sales (10,000 units @ $10)		$100,000		$100,000
Direct costs:				
Beginning inventory	$ 0		$ 0	
Direct materials (20,000 units @ $2.50)	50,000		50,000	
Direct labor (20,000 units @ $1.00)	20,000		20,000	
Variable overhead (20,000 units @ $1.50)	30,000		30,000	
Fixed mfg. overhead*			20,000	
Total	$100,000		$120,000	
Less inventory (10,000 units @ $5.00)	50,000			
10,000 @ $6.00			60,000	
Total variable costs		$ 50,000		
Contribution margin		$ 50,000		
Cost of sales				$ 60,000
Gross profit				$ 40,000
Selling and administrative expense	$ 30,000		30,000	
Fixed mfg. overhead*	20,000	$ 50,000		
Net profit for period		$ 0		$ 10,000

162

NOVEMBER

	Direct Costing		Absorption Costing	
Sales (25,000 @ $10)		$250,000		$250,000
Variable costs:				
Beginning inventory	$ 50,000		$ 60,000	
Direct materials (20,000 @ $2.50)	50,000		50,000	
Direct labor (20,000 @ $1.00)	20,000		20,000	
Variable overhead (20,000 @ $1.50)	30,000		30,000	
Fixed mfg. overhead*			30,000	
			20,000	
Total	$150,000		$180,000	
Less inventory (5,000 units @ $5.00)	25,000		5,000 @ $6.00	30,000
Total variable costs		$125,000		
Contribution margin		$125,000		
Cost of sales				$150,000
Gross profit				$100,000
Selling and administrative expense	$ 30,000			30,000
Fixed mfg. overhead*	20,000			
		$ 50,000		
Net profit for period		$ 75,000		$ 70,000

* Basically, it is the treatment of this important cost factor which distinguishes variable and absorption costing. If sales or administrative costs are variable, they would be included under that caption to the extent it is applicable.

Figure 13.1. Differences in reporting: direct costing and absorption costing

	Total Company	Plant X	Plant Y
Sales	2,000,000	1,200,000	800,000
Variable costs	1,200,000	660,000	540,000
Contribution margin	800,000	540,000	260,000
Controllable and identifiable fixed costs (advertising, sales, promotion, etc.)	300,000	200,000	100,000
Short-term margin	500,000	340,000	160,000
Noncontrollable and identifiable fixed costs (depreciation, taxes, etc.)	200,000	140,000	60,000
Long-term margin	300,000	200,000	100,000
Nonidentifiable fixed costs	100,000		
Net income	200,000		

Figure 13.2. Contribution margin approach: two plants

	Plant X	Product 1	Product 2	Product 3
Sales	1,200,000	500,000	400,000	300,000
Variable costs	660,000	300,000	200,000	160,000
Contribution margin	540,000	200,000	200,000	140,000
Controllable and identifiable fixed costs	160,000	60,000	50,000	50,000
Short-term margin	380,000	140,000	150,000	90,000
Noncontrollable and identifiable fixed costs	130,000	30,000	50,000	50,000
Long-term margin	250,000	110,000	100,000	40,000
Nonidentifiable fixed costs	50,000			
Net income	200,000			

Figure 13.3. Contribution margin: three products

Several advantages stem from the use of marginal costing concepts. The principal ones are:

1. The actual short- and long-run elements (the segments) of a diversified business are readily identifiable.

2. Essential decisions such as pricing or resource allocation can be made on hard facts compared with other hard facts, unclouded by estimates and irrelevant information.

3. Combined with the cost-volume analysis described in chapter 11, desirable volumes for individual products are readily determined.

CHAPTER **14**

Costs for Special Decisions

One of the most widely used measures of managerial ability is the return on investment obtained by the operation of a business. As will be seen in chapter 15, most business decisions involving investment are influenced by the rate of return estimated to be earned from each alternative. This chapter will be concerned with the selection of appropriate data for any given set of decisions—data that management can use to determine the best return on investment.

EVALUATION OF QUALITATIVE AND QUANTITATIVE FACTORS

Not all decisions are made on the basis of purely quantitative factors. For example, a business executive may become dissatisfied with the decor of his office and decide to repaint in the hope that this will give him a new outlook on his business. One might not deny the psychological advantage of a change in surroundings; however, it would be extremely difficult to quantify the financial advantages of such a paint job to the corporation.

For major decisions, an economic evaluation of the alternatives available should always be made, regardless of the qualitative factors. At the very least, such an economic evaluation would provide a foundation for the measurement of the intangible values. One should be very leery of a situation in which highly unfavorable tangible factors are outweighed by qualitative factors.

Interpreting Relevant Costs. In order to evaluate the quantitative factors in a given decision, the pertinent factors must first be isolated. Accounting records contain many costs; these are called *historical costs*. The fact that a cost is recorded, however, does not make it pertinent to a decision on future strategy. For example, assume that the firm has capitalized and is amortizing the money it expended to acquire a patent. The amount originally paid is called a sunk cost; no matter what the firm does in the present or the future, very little of the original expenditure can usually be recaptured by selling the asset. The amortization of the sunk cost is recorded as a cost against current operations, but the amount of such amortization is not pertinent to decisions regarding costs of future operations. Past costs, however, cannot be ignored entirely because they do serve as a guide to what can be expected in the future. The point is that they cannot simply be projected into the future because they occurred in the past.

The factors pertinent to a future decision are frequently called *relevant costs*. Relevant costs include some historical costs and some costs not yet incurred. The evaluation of their relevance is necessarily empirical in each situation. Relevant costs are to be distinguished from *opportunity costs*, which are the costs of alternate decisions. If one decides to buy a machine rather than to invest in bonds, the potential interest on the bonds is an opportunity cost. *Differential costs* are the pertinent costs for one decision minus the pertinent costs for an alternative decision.

ILLUSTRATION OF RELEVANT AND DIFFERENTIAL COSTS. Recently the Skider Corporation was approached by an outside service agency which proposed that it provide a repair and maintenance service. Figure 14.1 lists several costs, some of which are relevant and some of which are not.

The costs of direct labor, direct materials, and depreciation are not relevant to any decision on maintenance and repair; the costs of supplies, repairs and maintenance, indirect labor, and outside services are relevant.

Differential costs are illustrated in Figure 14.2.

Figure 14.2 indicates an advantage of $7,000 arising to the Skider Corporation if it were to use the outside agency for repairs and maintenance. If all other things were equal, meaning in this case the qualitative factors, it would behoove the Skider Corpora-

	Current Operation (company does own maintenance)	Service Contract	Identification of type of cost
Direct materials	$17,000	$17,000	Unavoidable
Direct labor	35,000	35,000	Unavoidable
Supplies	9,000	8,000	Different by $1,000
Repairs and maintenance	8,000	— 0 —	Different by $8,000
Indirect labor	11,000	7,000	Different by $4,000
Outside services	— 0 —	6,000	Different by $6,000
Depreciation	4,000	4,000	Sunk cost

Figure 14.1. Comparison of current operation and proposed alternative

Estimated decreases in cost:
Supplies	$1,000	
Repairs and maintenance	8,000	
Indirect labor	4,000	
Total estimated cost savings		$13,000
Less cost of outside service		6,000
Advantage of using outside service		$ 7,000

Figure 14.2. Comparison of differential costs to determine least cost maintenance decision

tion to take advantage of the service contract. The $7,000 quantifies the presently known relevant factors. Another way of stating relevant costs is on the basis of cash out of pocket in the future. The depreciation shown in Figure 14.1 represents cash out of pocket in the past, not in the future, and will not affect future cash flows. The costs of direct labor and direct materials are irrelevant to the decision.

CONSIDERATION OF LONG- AND SHORT-RUN COSTS. In the example given, the Skider Corporation was trying to decide between using an outside maintenance service and performing its own maintenance service for its manufacturing division on the basis of short-run costs. The figures used were the costs of only one year's operations. A more useful technique for making such a decision would be to view the alternatives over their entire lives and then compute the average annual savings or additional costs. It is important to remember: A decision that may appear to be very good in the short run may turn out to be very poor in the long run. For example, in Figure 14.2, if the cost of outside services were to go to $14,000 after two years and all other costs could be held constant, the choice would then switch back to the corporation's providing its own maintenance staff instead of using an outside service.

PAST OR SUNK COSTS. As shown above, past or sunk costs are irrelevant to a cost decision because they do not affect future out-of-pocket costs unless the assets they represent will be sold. If unamortized patent costs are carried on the books with a residual value of $25,000, with $5,000 to be amortized each year, the $5,000 is irrelevant. Assume that the patent can be sold for $10,000. The $10,000, plus any reduction in income taxes resulting from the $15,000 loss on disposal, is relevant. If the applicable tax rate is 50 percent, any projection involving the discontinuation of the product or process represented by the patent would necessarily include a $17,500 cash inflow as relevant:

Sale of patent right	$10,000
Tax reduction (50% of $15,000)	7,500
Relevant cost (reduction)	$17,500

TYPES OF SPECIAL DECISIONS

The typical decisions faced by management in which the special concepts discussed in this chapter are important are: (1) make or buy decisions, (2) buy or lease decisions, (3) decisions concerning expansion or combinations of businesses or product lines, and (4) decisions concerning the curtailment or dropping of businesses or product lines. This section will consider the types of information necessary for each of these decisions and illustrate the type of information needed for correct decisions.

The Make or Buy Decision. A decision manufacturers must face from time to time is whether to buy components or to make them. A related decision is whether to rent or purchase facilities. There are three major factors in such decisions. One is relative costs. Another is quality and quality control. The third is scheduling and the reliability of delivery so that assembly production is not interrupted. A work stoppage in the plant of a supplier of a relatively minor part could bring production to a halt. The location of substitute sources of supply can be extremely expensive.

Frequently a company will manufacture part of its need for a component and farm out the rest. This practice has two advantages. First, it tends to keep both the supplier and the internal source honest in terms of cost and quality because each knows it is competing with the other. Second, it provides elasticity in capacity if wide swings in demand are common. No hard-and-fast rules can be laid down; the relevance of the various factors depends on the context of each decision at the point when it must be made.

One factor to consider in any decision would be the availability of idle facilities. If idle facilities can be put to another and better use than to make the parts, it would seem that the company should not make its own parts, unless the return on investment is such that investment in additional facilities is warranted. But if that is the case, why are there idle facilities in the first place? In any event, this investment becomes a capital budgeting decision, as discussed in chapter 15.

Assume that the Skider Corporation uses a subassembly called widgets in its manufacturing process. The cost of manufacturing the widgets on a per unit basis is shown below.

	Per Unit
Direct labor	$2.00
Direct materials	1.00
Variable overhead	3.00
Identifiable fixed overhead	1.50
Allocated joint fixed overhead	2.00
	$9.50

The cost of manufacturing widgets for the Skider Corporation is $9.50. If the company were approached by an outside organization that promised to manufacture the widgets for them for $9.00 per unit, would it be profitable for the Skider Corporation to accept the outside offer?

At first, it would appear that since $9.00 is less than $9.50 per unit, it would be advantageous for the Skider Corporation to subcontract these widgets. However, an analysis of the last two factors, identifiable fixed overhead and allocated joint fixed overhead, would lead to a different answer. If the identifiable fixed overhead did not change (in other words, it would still be the same amount regardless of whether or not the company manufactured widgets), that fixed overhead is not a relevant cost, and the relevant cost of manufacturing widgets is now reduced to $8.00. Furthermore, it is highly unlikely that allocated joint fixed overhead would be reduced by the elimination of the widget manufacturing operation. This means that the relevant costs of manufacturing widgets would be reduced even further, possibly as low as $6.00. On this basis it does not appear profitable for the Skider Corporation to accept the outside offer. However, there are other factors to be considered. For example, if the Skider Corporation had no plans to use the space made idle by discontinuing the manufacture of widgets, this decision would seem to be sound. On the other hand, if it could put the space to good use, the additional profits generated by that space might more than offset the additional cost of subcontracting the material.

The Buy or Lease Decision. Another management decision is whether to lease or to buy. An example would be whether to buy a computer system outright or to lease it for a specified number of years. This decision differs from the make/buy decision in that it is complicated by the time value of money. In the purchase alternative, there would most likely be a substantial cash down payment required in the year of acquisition, while in a lease situation more or less equal payments would be required over the life of the machine. This complication is discussed in more detail in chapter 15.

Business Expansion or Combination. One of the more pleasant problems facing companies from time to time is expansion. A major problem in connection with expansion is that if sales volume exceeds the normal productive capacity, measures may have to be taken to increase capacity. There are several ways of increasing capacity and output. The first way available to most companies is to utilize plant and equipment more than one shift per day. Some industries make standard use of a three-shift operation; others make standard use of a two-shift operation for production and use the third shift for maintenance and repairs; still others are wedded to the idea of operating on only one shift.

To examine the potential consequences to a firm currently operating on a one-shift basis and wishing to expand to a two-shift basis, let us look at Figure 14.3.

SKIDER CORPORATION
INCOME STATEMENT

	Most Recent Year	Incremental Revenues and Costs
Sales	$400,000	$300,000
Cost of goods manufactured and sold		
Direct materials	$200,000	$150,000
Direct labor	80,000	80,000
Variable overhead	40,000	33,000
Fixed overhead	30,000	3,000
Total costs of goods manufactured and sold	$350,000	$266,000
Net income from manufacturing	$ 50,000	$ 34,000

Figure 14.3. Examination of data to decide whether or not to expand operations to a second shift

We see from Figure 14.3 that the Skider Corporation is currently operating at a net income from manufacturing of $50,000. Its sales department has made very optimistic forecasts based on firm orders for additional business. Company management is convinced that the company can sell an additional 100,000 units at $3 per unit. After some careful examination of the facts, management has concluded that expanding operations to a second shift would increase costs by $266,000. On this basis it would appear that if sales are $300,000 and incremental costs only $266,000, the company should go ahead and expand operations to a second shift. Of course, this assumes that there is no additional cost for selling or administration of the business. But this is not the whole story; it is only the examination of one alternative. If there is any additional investment required, the $34,000 incremental return must be related to that additional investment. Again, this becomes a capital budgeting problem and is covered more thoroughly in chapter 15.

Business Curtailment. All too frequently, businesses are faced not with problems of expansion but with problems of curtailment. Many times a product line will not carry its own weight in terms of profitability. When this occurs, management must make the decision of whether or not to drop the product line. One factor that would have to be considered in such a decision would be whether this is a temporary or permanent decline in profitability. Another factor would be the tie-in between the sales of this product and the sales of other products. It is important to remember that in determining whether or not to drop a product line, differential costs are the costs to be considered. If a product line is unprofitable because of the allocation of joint-product costs to it but the revenues generated by the line exceed its differential costs, dropping it would further decrease profits. Where the facilities used for the unprofitable line could be put to use on more profitable items, an exception to the foregoing arises. If the return from the alternative uses exceeds the return from the product line in question, the product line should be dropped.

Figure 14.4 illustrates the type of analysis that would be undertaken to determine whether or not the product line should be dropped.

In examining Figure 14.4, two facts should become apparent immediately. The first is that the statement is prepared on a contribution margin basis; that is, each department or product line is matched with its revenue against its direct expenses. Any joint expenses are not allocated to the individual product line. This comparison is developed to determine whether each product

SKIDER CORPORATION
INCOME STATEMENT

TYPICAL YEAR

	Total	Widgets	Product Lines Gidgets	Didgets
Net sales	$650,000	$300,000	$200,000	$150,000
Direct costs of sales:				
Cost of goods sold	$400,000	$160,000	$130,000	$110,000
Variable selling costs	50,000	30,000	10,000	10,000
Variable administrative costs	50,000	20,000	15,000	15,000
Total variable costs	$500,000	$210,000	$155,000	$135,000
Product line fixed costs	55,000	20,000	18,000	17,000
Total costs	$555,000	$230,000	$173,000	$152,000
Contribution margin	$95,000	$ 70,000	$ 27,000	$ (2,000)
Joint fixed costs	$28,000			
Net income	$67,000			

Figure 14.4

line can cover its own costs. Note, too, that there can be separate fixed costs for each product line, as well as joint fixed costs. In the example in Figure 14.4, the product line of didgets should be discontinued because it does not produce enough revenues to cover its direct costs. If, however, evidence can be developed to show that this product line contributes to the profitable sales of other product lines, it might well be necessary to continue to manufacture and sell didgets. It should also be noted that if the didget line were eliminated, total profits would increase from $67,000 to $69,000. Were it determined that $3,000 of the didget product line fixed costs could not be eliminated by dropping the line, it would be unwise to eliminate didgets.

There are many other examples of executive decisions that can be made using differential cost data. The accountant's problem in every case is to determine which data are relevant for each decision and to provide management with that information in an understandable format so that it can make the best decision under the circumstances.

CHAPTER 15

Capital Budgeting

The budgets which have been discussed in earlier chapters have all been budgets of expenses, that is, costs written off against revenues of the current year or carried over to another year as part of inventories. Budgeting techniques are equally applicable to decision making involving the acquisition of capital goods or the undertaking of certain projects, for example, an advertising campaign. As with the budgeting of expenses, budgeting for capital or project expenditures relies mainly on a prediction of future events and is only as strong as such a prediction.

Several different methods, ranging from rule-of-thumb to the highly esoteric, are used in making projections of capital and special project needs. No matter how scientific the method of capital budgeting, the most important factor bearing on a decision is a reasonably accurate forecast of future events. The forecast itself may be made in a totally unscientific manner, since so much of future demand is based on whim, style, and the unforeseen. Any decision that would be rejected if a small change were to occur in any aspect of the related forecast should be more carefully examined, especially in terms of the critical factors in the forecast.

Emergency Method. Certain equipment expenditures are normally made only when the item to be replaced is no longer functional. The simplest example of this type of expenditure is the replacement of a transistor radio battery only after it has completely failed to function, in spite of long warnings in the form of inferior performance. Little, if any, planning is involved in such a replacement. However, we are usually not so unfortunate as to have a general collapse such as that of the "One

Hoss Shay." Where machine tools and buildings are involved, waiting for a general collapse before planning replacements would eventually put a company out of business. A further criticism of the emergency method is that it applies, at best, only to replacements; expansion and new projects simply cannot be accommodated under such a method.

The Persuasion Method. The *persuasion method* of making capital or project expenditures follows the old proverb of the squeaking wheel getting the grease. Under this method, the most persuasive individual sells his needs or projects regardless of whether these provide the optimum use of resources by the firm. In the age of the computer, with operations-research techniques and the scientific methods of evaluation described later in this book, persuasion is thought to be outmoded and unscientific. However, one must realize that many of the assumptions implicit in the mathematical techniques about to be described are themselves inexact. Because of this, it can be argued that the point of persuasion has moved from the point of presentation of the project to the point of the analysis of the details leading to the project. It would be well to remember that any decision has critical factors and that such critical factors should be examined to determine their sensitivity to changes in assumptions.

Return-of-Capital Method. The simplest of the mathematical methods used is the determination of the time span, frequently called the payback period, over which the capital outlay will be recovered. Recovery is defined in terms of cost reductions or net revenue increases, which have the same effect on net profits. Thus, if the $10,000 cost of a capital outlay results in $2,500 annual increased profitability, the payback period is four years.

$$\frac{\text{Cost}}{\text{Savings}} = \frac{\$10,000}{\$\ 2,500} = 4 \text{ years}$$

There is some disagreement among authorities as to whether accrual or cash methods of accounting should be used in computing the savings. The more rational view, apparently, is to use the cash method, omitting depreciation from the calculation, because depreciation is only a technique designed to allocate the cost of a capital asset over the time period of its expected use. If the machine that was to be replaced by the $10,000 expenditure had a book value of $4,000 that was being amortized using straight-line depreciation over a remaining life of four years, the sale of the old machine would still provide only that cash flow equal to the proceeds of the sale. If the machine is not sold, the cash flow from that unused machine is zero. The cash flow is not to be confused with the $1,000 annual depreciation charge which is a noncash expense. The new machine would also provide an annual depreciation charge. In the same period, the $10,000 replacement would have provided $10,000 cash flow, recovering its cost. For the time being, both illustrations ignore tax considerations.

Income-Tax Consideration. The above explanation of how the return-of-capital method works is oversimplified because it ignores income taxes and the cost of the capital used for the project or capital expenditure. In computing the annual cash savings, the tax on these savings or tax cost of a particular decision must be considered. It is impossible to compute the tax saving without considering the effect of depreciation on the taxes. Accordingly, at this point depreciation should be considered in the analysis. If our new $10,000 machine were depreciated over ten years on a straight-line basis, assuming a 50 percent tax rate, no salvage value for the machine, and no investment credit, the annual savings would be only $1,750 as calculated below.

Annual cash savings	$ 2,500
Less: Depreciation for tax purposes	1,000
Increase in taxable income	$ 1,500
Income tax	750
Income after tax	$ 750
Add: Depreciation	1,000
Net annual cash savings	$ 1,750
Time span for return of capital	$\dfrac{\$10,000}{1,750} = 5.71$ years

This saving must then be weighed against risk and the cost of money.

The principal criticism levied against this method of making a capital expenditure decision is that it contemplates no profits.

Presumably the risk of investment will be taken only when the payback will be completed in a short and foreseeable time. In making a choice, it would be natural to favor that project providing the shortest payback period. But the purpose of making a capital investment is to make a profit, not merely to break even. If the anticipated life of the investment is substantially greater than the payback period used to compute its viability, the return-of-capital method is faced with fewer objections.

Comparative Salvage Value: A Safety Factor. Inasmuch as the savings generated by a capital investment project is only one factor to be considered, it is argued that the project with the most profit potential should be favored. If risks are equal, such favoritism is common sense. More often than not, however, the more profit potential, the riskier the project. Therefore, a comparison of projects that uses the return-of-capital method along with an estimate of salvage or bail out probabilities at various stages might well be worthwhile. Assume two projects with equal capital requirements but with unequal payback periods and unequal salvage possibilities at several different time stages. In this context, salvage means the net value that could be realized on liquidation of the project.

In Figure 15.1, the salvage values given are as of the end of each year. The potential loss is the capital outlay, minus the sum of the accumulated cash inflows and the anticipated year-end salvage value. Project A, while the payback in it is less, also shows smaller potential losses in the earlier years. Project B, with its higher ratio of return, appears to be very risky in early years.

Rate-of-Return Method. Mathematically, the reciprocal of the payback method is termed the *rate-of-return method*. Thus, the rate of return on Project A in Figure 15.1 is 10 percent.

$$\frac{\text{Annual Return}}{\text{Capital Investment}} = \frac{\$\ 10,000}{\$100,000} = 10\%$$

On Project B the rate of return is 25 percent.

$$\frac{\text{Annual Return}}{\text{Capital Investment}} = \frac{\$\ 25,000}{\$100,000} = 25\%$$

Some argue that the capital investment should be shown at one-half the actual amount because, assuming a uniform rate of

Project A

| | Cost | $100,000 |
| | Payback | $ 10,000 annually for 25 years |

	Salvage Value	Potential Loss
End of first year	$80,000	$10,000
Second year	70,000	10,000
Third year	60,000	10,000
Fourth year	50,000	10,000
Fifth year	40,000	10,000

Project B

| | Cost | $100,000 |
| | Payback | $ 25,000 annually for 15 years |

	Salvage Value	Potential Loss
End of first year	$25,000	$50,000
Second year	5,000	45,000
Third year	0	25,000
Fourth year	0	0

Figure 15.1. Comparison of safety factors

depreciation, only one-half the capital is committed in an average year. Obviously, it is relatively unimportant which method is used in comparing projections as long as a consistent basis is employed. Of course, if a project with uniform recovery is compared with a form of investment, bonds, for example, where capital is recovered at the end of the investment period, such a variance should be considered.

Accounting Method. A variation of the rate-of-return method, sometimes called the *accounting method*, is frequently used to project balance sheets from year to year, using alternative investments. Where the rate of return is at differing rates from year to year, or investment possibilities other than internally used capital are available, this method has much to recommend it. Most certainly the time devoted to proof where a major project is involved might well be worthwhile.

The criticism is often made that the accounting method contemplates only investments in fixed assets or other balance sheet items and is not appropriate to gauge investments in advertising or research and development. This hardly seems to be a valid criticism, however, if reasonable forecasts of the results of such expenditures can be made. The point is that all methods of projecting are subject to the guesses and persuasive efforts of their advocates.

Discounted-Cash-Flow Method. The most scientific method of gauging the desirability of a particular project is to treat the annual savings as an annuity. Referring again to the discussion of the return-of-capital method, the criticism was levied that it is a zero game because profitability is ignored. If two projects cost the same and show the same annual return of capital, obviously the project that contemplates the longer period of payback is the preferred one.

The rate of return on capital has been described as the rental for the use of money. If the firm has funds available or access to funds either through additional equity or from borrowing, profit maximization would result from the selection of the highest rate of return commensurate with safety until the cost of the additional borrowing exceeds the return promised by the marginal project. Another way to suboptimally handle the problem is to consider only those projects that afford a predetermined rate of return on capital, along with the recovery of capital. The resolution of the problem requires some familiarity with the principles of annuities.

An annuity is the recovery of capital invested, plus compound interest, over a time-span. Figure 15.2 indicates that one can purchase an annuity of $2,309.75 for $10,000 if the terms of the annuity are a 5 percent rate of return and the recovery of capital in five years.

The proof that this is so follows (figures rounded).

Year	Beginning of Year	Interest	Payout	End of Year
1	$10,000	$500	$2,310	$8,190
2	8,190	410	2,310	6,290
3	6,290	315	2,310	4,295
4	4,295	215	2,310	2,200
5	2,200	110	2,310	0

It follows that one can choose between projects or test them against a predetermined rate simply by using the appropriate

Time Period	5%	6%	7%
1	1.050000	1.060000	1.070000
2	.537805	.545437	.553092
3	.367209	.374110	.381052
4	.282012	.288592	.295228
5	.230975	.237396	.243891
6	.197018	.203863	.209796
7	.172820	.179135	.185553
8	.154722	.161036	.167468
9	.140690	.147022	.153487
10	.129505	.135868	.142378
11	.120389	.126793	.133357
12	.112825	.119277	.125902
13	.106456	.112960	.119651
14	.101024	.107585	.114345
15	.096342	.102963	.109795

Figure 15.2. Periodic payment required to amortize $1 and interest

table. Assume a predetermined rate of 6 percent, a project costing $5,000, and an expected savings of $600 per year for ten years. Interpolating to $1 and referring to Figure 15.2, we find an annual cash inflow of $.12 per year. Our table indicates this to be below our sought after 6 percent rate of return, and the project is abandoned. As a matter of fact, the rate of return in the rejected project is slightly less than 3 percent per annum.

The reciprocal of the table shown in Figure 15.2 is the present value of an annuity. That is, the right to receive $2,310 per year for five years, assuming a 5 percent rate of return, has a present value of $10,000. Figure 15.3 is a table of the present value of an annuity of $1, and we find that $2,310 multiplied by 4.329, the factor for 5 percent for five years, is $10,000.

Therefore, we can determine the attractiveness of a particular project in terms of its present value by using rates of return high enough to include a risk factor and the consequences of possible changes in the tax rate. Changes in the tax rate would include changes in allowable depreciation methods and the availability of an investment credit. The rates that have been used to illustrate the principles of annuities are far too low for this purpose. Figure 15.4 shows the present value of an annuity of $1 at a 25 percent rate of return.

Time Period	5%	6%
1	.9524	.9434
2	1.8594	1.8333
3	2.7320	2.6730
4	3.5460	3.4651
5	4.3294	4.2124
6	5.0775	4.9173
7	5.7864	5.5824
8	6.4632	6.2098
9	7.1078	6.8017
10	7.7217	7.3601
11	8.3064	7.8869
12	8.8633	8.3838
13	9.3936	8.8527
14	9.8986	9.2950
15	10.3797	9.7122

Figure 15.3. Present value of an annuity of $1

No ten-year project can cost more than $3,571 for each $1,000 anticipated annual return and maintain the required 25 percent rate of return on capital invested. Such a rate of return, incidentally, is by no means unrealistic.

Time Period	25%
1	.800
2	1.440
3	1.952
4	2.362
5	2.689
6	2.951
7	3.161
8	3.329
9	3.463
10	3.571
11	3.656
12	3.725
13	3.780
14	3.824
15	3.859

*Figure 15.4. Present value of an annuity of $1
at a 25 percent rate of return*

CHAPTER 16

Nonmanufacturing Costs

Without doubt, the field of nonmanufacturing costs represents the great unexplored and uncharted area in cost accounting. In general, this field covers selling, administrative, and research expenses. While techniques from modern theories of budgeting and standard costing are readily transferable to the nonmanufacturing area, the problem, simply stated, is to find a base against which to measure variances from standard. If steel costs $125 per ton, a ton of products made from steel must cost at least $125 for materials. But against what standard can or should a company measure the cost of the research and development leading to the design of the product, the cost of selling it, and the cost of warehousing and distribution? For the company as a whole, what is a good standard for measuring the efficiency of the cost accounting department?

ADMINISTRATIVE COSTS

The most commonly used method of deciding what are proper costs for administrative functions is to follow last year's expenses and to take into consideration the competence, bargaining power, and ability of the manager of the particular administrative function. Such a method usually leads to a rigid and bureaucratic operation. Change obviously decreases stability, and stability of operations is frequently mistaken for efficiency. Thus, it would seem that reliance on the manager's good judgment is a necessity. Unfortunately, all too often the manager's position is rated on the basis of the number of people who work for him. The larger the base of the pyramid, the larger the salary of the top block. As Juvenal said almost 2,000 years ago, "But who will guard the guardians?"

Fixed and Variable Costs. Administrative costs, like any other costs, can be broken down into their respective categories of fixed and variable expenses. Such division does not deal with the efficiency of operations; nevertheless, a very useful purpose may still be served. For example, certain positions and other expenses in the cost accounting department would probably be classified as variable. If production is at 80 percent of normal level, should not some of the costs of the cost accounting department be reduced by 20 percent? After all, the detail to be accounted for has dropped by that amount. Rarely, if ever, can such administrative costs respond to variable cost concepts as factory costs can. Most administrative costs represent people or expensive equipment, both of which are added in sizable increments. For example, if there are six clerks in the cost accounting department who are properly classified as variable, it is impossible to cut back precisely 20 percent. The same problem would arise, obviously, if the department rented four remote terminals for its electronic data processing equipment.

Work Measurement. It is widely held that objective standards can be developed against which the efficiency of certain types of work can be measured. A norm for a typist might be so many invoices or letters per day; for a warehouseman, so many tons of merchandise handled or orders filled in the warehouse. Such norms are always subject to the criticism that the work performed is routine only by description. Thus, a typist who transcribes complex legal or medical terms might very well have a lower page output than one who types simpler matter, although it might be possible to develop a regression model to relate these factors and therefore set some sort of standards for each. How does one measure the efficiency of an accounting clerk? To attempt such a measurement by numbers posted or papers handled would accomplish little besides the hiring of more workers.

Very likely the most valid criticism of work measurement techniques is that they start with the assumption that the job itself is necessary and question only whether that job is performed adequately. In many situations, the appropriate question is the need for the job. The analogy is to the economy of flying coach on a trip that need not have been made. There is a great amount of literature in the field, but little of it sheds any real light on the basic question of how to establish a work standard for nonroutine operations. Perhaps the only valid standard is a dollar value set on the department's function, leaving to the managers the detail of how to perform that function.

RESEARCH AND DEVELOPMENT COSTS

It has been suggested that each of the three methods of setting standards for administrative costs, supervisory discretion, fixed and variable analysis, and work measurement, is inherently unsatisfactory. All the methods are good when compared with any attempt to set standards for research and development activities. Even the question of whether research and development expenditures should be expensed or capitalized is moot.

Some writers suggest distributing the costs of research and development over all the manufacturing departments. The theory of such action is that all managers should be aware of the importance and cost of this function even though they cannot control its cost. Such action, however, does not help with the basic question of the standard against which to measure research and development costs. Frequently, research and development costs are budgeted as a percentage of anticipated sales and in this manner are controlled only in terms of spending totals. The conceptual difficulty with such an approach is that it reduces research and development expenditures when sales fall off, which may be the very point at which additional effort should be exerted. The rebuttal to this argument is that it does not follow that the firm automatically achieves faster or better results simply by spending more for research and development.

DISTRIBUTION COSTS

The costs incurred in getting the product to the customer after its manufacture or purchase are in some degree measurable against either a quantitative or a monetary standard. Thus, the costs of stocking shelves and racks in a discount store can be measured against sales volume or number of items handled. However, whether the operation is retail distribution or warehousing, the same problems in distributing costs to a multiplicity of products exist as in manufacturing.

Essentially the same techniques used in direct costing can be applied to distribution costs. Assume that a retailer stocks 10,000 different items. What are the profits on each item? To which items should more shelf or display space be given? The problem is illustrated in Figure 16.1.

Two questions are raised by Figure 16.1. First, is the distribution of floor space on the basis of square feet occupied a realistic index of measurement? Second, if Product E is discontinued, will sales of other products be affected? There is really no accurate answer to either question; however, the question illustrates the kind of probing that can lead to greater profits in distributing products.

This last point can be further emphasized by using the same figures as those used in Figure 16.1 and assigning costs proportionate to the sales of the individual products. Assigning costs to products on the basis of their sales, although widely done, contains a basic fallacy, as will be demonstrated in Figures 16.2 and 16.3. If sales were used as the basis of distributing the floor space cost, a contribution margin analysis would so indicate.

	Total	Product A	B	C	D	E
Sales	$10,000	$2,500	$2,500	$2,500	$1,500	$1,000
Cost of product	6,500	1,750	1,500	1,800	750	700
Contribution margin	$ 3,500	$ 750	$1,000	$ 700	$ 750	$ 300
Floor space cost*	2,000	400	400	400	400	400
Gross income	$ 1,500	$ 350	$ 600	$ 300	$ 350	$ (100)
Other expenses	500					
Profit	$ 1,000					

* Each product uses the same square footage.

Figure 16.1. Contribution margin approach to distribution costs

	Total	A	B	C	D	E
				Product		
		A	B	C	D	E
Sales	$10,000	$2,500	$2,500	$2,500	$1,500	$1,000
Cost of product	6,500	1,750	1,500	1,800	750	700
Contribution margin	$ 3,500	$ 750	$1,000	$ 700	$ 750	$ 300
Floor space cost*	2,000	500	500	500	300	200
Gross income	$ 1,500	$ 250	$ 500	$ 200	$ 450	$ 100
Other expenses	500					
Profit	$ 1,000					

* 2,000/10,000 or 20 percent of sales.

Figure 16.2. Costs distributed as a percentage of sales

PRODUCT B

	Total	A	B	C	D
			Product		
Sales	$11,500	$2,500	$5,000	$2,500	$1,500
Cost of product	7,300	1,750	3,000	1,800	750
Contribution margin	$ 4,200	$ 750	$2,000	$ 700	$ 750
Floor space cost	2,000				
Gross income	$ 2,200				

PRODUCT D

	Total	A	B	C	D
Sales	$10,500	$2,500	$2,500	$2,500	$3,000
Cost of product	6,550	1,750	1,500	1,800	1,500
Contribution margin	$ 3,950	$ 750	$1,000	$ 700	$1,500
Floor space cost	2,000				
Gross income	$ 1,950				

Figure 16.3. Double sales of Product B and D respectively

Assuming that Product E can be dropped without hurting sales of other products and that sales of other products can be expanded indefinitely, the analysis in Figure 16.1 indicates:

Product B   600/2,500 = 24% Gross income
Product D   350/1,500 = 23.3% Gross income

Figure 16.2, on the other hand, indicates:

> Product B   500/2,500 = 20% Gross income
> Product D   450/1,500 = 30% Gross income

Proof of the fallacy of distributing costs using sales as the base is shown by dropping Product E and increasing the sales of either Product B or Product D as in Figure 16.3.

Mathematical techniques are available to aid in the determination of the optimum product mix and of space allocation. These are explained in more detail in chapter 19 in the discussion of linear programming.

SALES COSTS

All the problems of work measurement and cost allocation discussed in connection with distribution, administrative, and research and development costs are present in connection with the costs of obtaining sales. Here, again, the only rational approach is on the basis of the marginal contribution, always bearing in mind that the customer who has come into the store as a result of a promotion on winter underwear may, as the result of a display or other inducement to impulse buying, also purchase a refrigerator. Again, the allocation of costs based on the dollar value of sales is an extremely dangerous practice and can lead to concentration of effort in areas of lesser profitability. See chapter 14 on costs for special decisions for the concepts to use in deciding whether to expand or contract a particular product line.

CHAPTER 17

Managerial Cost Systems and the Impact of Electronic Data Processing

Cost accounting systems can be designed and installed by anyone. However, top management should designate and approve the objectives desired from the system. Top management should determine the type of costing to be used, the reports to be issued, the use to be made of those reports, and the accounting procedures to be followed. In such matters as inventory control and costing, depreciation methods, and the treatment of research and development costs, major policy considerations are involved.

One of the prime uses of the cost accounting system is reporting and controlling the operations of subordinate managers; therefore, top management must pay careful attention to the objectives of the system. If a haphazard collection of procedures is thrown together, the resulting chaos will not lend itself to managerial efficiency.

DESIGNING A SYSTEM

Before designing a system, top management must decide what type of cost accounting system is to be used: job order or process, historical or standard cost.

It is important to remember that accounting is fundamentally a communications medium. If management is to use the information developed by the cost accountant for decision making, the information must be received by management in time to make the decision. Furthermore, the information must be clear and concise so it can be readily digested and understood.

Management by Exception. One of the fundamental concepts of modern-day management is *management by exception*. A good cost accounting system will be designed to spotlight exceptions by focusing attention on situations and areas that deviate from plans or normal conditions. The reasoning behind this is that with limited time at its disposal, management should focus on those things which are not satisfactory. As discussed in the chapter on standard costs, when there are variances within a given range, those variances should be pinpointed for particular managerial action.

It should not be inferred from this that the results of ordinary operations are not important. Naturally, these are important, but by concentrating on the exceptions, management is best able to concentrate on problems that need the most attention.

Internal Control. Internal controls are many and varied. It is probably best to discuss the controls appropriate to an accounting system in terms of three major categories under internal control: personnel, responsibility and authority, and checks and balances. The American Institute of Certified Public Accountants defines internal control as ". . . the plan of organization and all of the coordinate methods and measures adopted within a business to safeguard its assets, check the accuracy and reliability of its accounting data, promote operational efficiency, and encourage adherence to prescribed managerial policies."[1]

For the cost accountant, the last three items are particularly important. The accounting data must be accurate and reliable within a given range. The system should be designed to operate efficiently, not only in gathering its own data but also in coordinating the tasks of the people who work within the system. Finally, the accounting system should be one that encourages adherence to prescribed policy.

PERSONNEL. The prime task of any accounting system is to determine that the employees utilized by the business are adequate for the purpose. Employing people adequate for the purpose does not mean an employer should use the lowest cost personnel available, unless one uses a long-run definition of low costs.

---

[1] Committee on Auditing Procedures, Auditing Standards and Procedures, American Institute of Certified Public Accountants, 1963, p. 27.

No matter how well designed a system is, the designer can be sure that one or more persons will find methods of circumventing his built-in internal controls. The best protection against embezzlement or defalcation is to hire honest people. Also, no person should be assigned to a task that he does not have the ability to perform. It is equally bad to assign high-powered individuals to low-powered jobs. They soon become bored with simple tasks, and their work suffers.

LINES OF AUTHORITY AND RESPONSIBILITY. There are several reasons for assigning responsibility and authority to subordinates. A person who is told to do a job and is given the responsibility for that job will not perform adequately if he has not been given the requisite authority. Similarly, a person who is given the authority to perform but is not held responsible for his performance will likely do his job inadequately. Just the act of assigning responsibility to individuals has a psychological impact that tends to promote better work from them.

BUILT-IN CHECKS AND BALANCES. Good personnel and clearly distinguished lines of authority and responsibility for those personnel are substantial parts of an internal control system. However, these are not enough. There must also be built-in checks and balances to guard against improper performance. One of these built-in checks and balances is the separation of record keeping and asset handling. For example, the person who purchases materials should not be the same person who keeps the accounting records of materials on hand, and neither of them should have the responsibility for making periodic counts of materials on hand.

Other features of a good internal control system are the bonding of individuals who handle cash or inventories, the requirement that they take vacations, and the rotation of duties among them. Another check is to have all transactions recorded immediately, fully, and in such a manner as to make it difficult for an employee to commit a fraud. Prenumbered documents and special recording devices help here. Subjecting the output of various individuals to the scrutiny of an outside certified public accountant or a special internal auditor serves as an additional control feature.

THE IMPACT OF ELECTRONIC DATA PROCESSING

Probably most businesses still operate under a cost accounting system designed while the company was using manual accounting procedures, even though they have installed a computer; the only difference between the old and the new is the design and processing of the various forms. The result is that outmoded systems are processed more rapidly, frequently an aggravation of an existing bad situation. It would be far better for such companies to start from scratch and design entirely new systems to process their data when they obtain a computer. In fact, many in the field of systems design feel that most of the savings from installing computers will come about because of a redesigned system rather than the actual use of the computer. Where it is properly utilized, the computer is a godsend because of its unique operating characteristics.

The main thrust of electronic data processing on the accounting process is in the primary processing of high-volume records. Computer printouts of journals representing the transactions of a major retailer are a very expensive feature of electronic data processing systems, one that many systems experts decry as unnecessary. A great deal more data can be contained and maintained without being printed out, and this wealth of information is always available for call-up by many users in the company.

Characteristics of the Computer. Under a mechanical or manual accounting system all data is in written or printed form and is easily checked by auditors or cost accountants. However, before a given entry can be utilized, the page on which the entry has been made must first be found. Furthermore, the totals from an individual page can be footed only horizontally or vertically. Summaries of several pages can only extend the horizontal and vertical dimensions.

The computer, on the other hand, does not leave a trail that can be read by an untrained person unless it is specifically programmed to leave that trail. Creating such a trail as a normal routine is an expensive process; therefore, the computer is usually programmed to print out only the exceptions to or deviations from plans. The computer does, however, permit instantaneous access to individual entries and footings in any conceivable pattern: horizontal, vertical, parabola, zigzag, and so forth. Furthermore, analytical material can be furnished in three dimensions. While the traditional checks and balances of internal control are not available where the computer is used, many other measures of control can be incorporated directly into the program of computer instructions.

Operating Functions of the Computer. There are basically five essential characteristics of the operating functions of the computer. They are input, storage, arithmetic-logic, control, and output.

INPUT. Before the computer can solve any problems, it must receive the necessary facts. Any data and instructions involving the processing of the facts must also be put into the computer in some usable form. There are a number of devices that will perform such an input function, and new ones are constantly being developed and marketed. Generally, they take the form of direct man-machine communication without the necessity of an input medium, for example, a remote time-sharing station. Or there is indirect communication through the media of punch cards or punch tape. Regardless of the device used, all such instruments are considered to be input between man and machine.

This is perhaps the weakest part of the entire computer complex. In recognition of this weakness an acronym, GIGO, has arisen, which stands for "garbage in, garbage out." In other words, no matter how good your processing with the computer, if the proper data is not fed into the computer no usable answer can come out.

STORAGE. All computer installations depend on the central processing unit, sometimes called the "black box" or CPU. The storage control and arithmetic-logic units are located within such a unit. There are four major purposes for the storage center of the central processor, three of which relate to the actual processing of the data. First, data are held in the storage area until they are ready to be processed. Second, additional storage space is utilized for holding data being processed and for retaining intermediate results of such processing. Third, the finished product is held in storage until it is released in the form of output information. Fourth, the storage unit also holds the program instructions until they are needed.

ARITHMETIC-LOGIC. The arithmetic-logic section of the CPU is where all calculations are performed and all decisions are made. The information being processed comes from the storage section to the arithmetic-logic section and returns to the storage section during the processing operation. No process is performed in the storage location.

CONTROL. The control unit acts as a coordinating center for the component parts of the computer. It selects, interprets, and executes the program instructions to control all the other parts of the computer. The control unit itself does not perform any actual processing operations on the data; it works on the units that do perform such operations.

OUTPUT. The output function, like the input function, is a means of communication between machine and man. The output devices take information in machine-coded form and convert it to man-usable form.

Advantages of the Computer. Where there is a tremendous volume of data to be processed, or where there is a long, complicated, repetitive type of problem, it is much faster and cheaper to record and update this material with a computer than by any other means.

In terms of the accounting function, the major use made of computers has been for routine, clerical-type tasks such as accounts receivable, accounts payable, payroll, and inventory control. However, the computer has many more advantages than the mere ability to process a greater volume of data more accurately and more reliably than any manual or mechanical means. With proper programming, the machine can perform a variety of analyses from any source document, the cost of such special analyses being reduced dramatically with regular usage. The computer can read, write, compare, and transfer information from one location to another. Because of these practical abilities, computers are valuable tools for solving all sorts of planning and control problems, particularly those that recur frequently or that involve substantial outlays of money.

Applications of the Computer to Cost Accounting Problems

and Systems. Several refineries in the oil industry mix their crude oils and change temperature and pressure applications to vary the output of their processing in accordance with current market information as to prices of the various end products. Such constant updating, which maximizes profitability, is possible only with computer use.

As discussed in chapter 8, the computer is widely used in the application of overhead to various departments to determine product costs. It is also frequently used in distribution cost analysis to determine whether selling certain products to certain customers is profitable. A manufacturer can feed information into a computer concerning purchase and uses of materials, related costs, and the beginning inventory balance. The computer can store the information, update it with subsequent transactions, and recall and imprint the summary of all inventory information whenever desired. It can also be programmed to advise the firm when a particular product reaches a reorder point. Many of the quantitative techniques discussed in chapter 19, including statistical methods in operations research, could not be performed without using the computer due to limitations in time and manpower.

With the basic information available from its use as a storage bin for sales, payroll, inventory, and related data, the special-purpose uses of the computer are as varied as the ingenuity of the users.

CHAPTER 18

Profit Centers and Transfer Prices

There has been a substantial movement toward larger and more complex business organizations over the past two or three decades. With this growth and complexity have arisen a whole new series of problems in measuring the results of operations, rewarding the operating managers, and setting goals for the organization. To account effectively for operations of the more complex businesses, it has been necessary to divide operations into divisions or departments and to designate people to be responsible for them.

The typical business uses the department as a basis of control and reward of the responsible manager. It is therefore necessary to have accounting systems that gather meaningful information on the activities of the departments so the departmental management can be evaluated.

Responsibility and Controllability. Although some attempts have been made to separate controllability and responsibility in accounting for costs and profits, it appears impossible to have one without the other. Controllable expenses are subject to the authority and responsibility of a specific individual or responsibility center. Care must be exercised in classifying an expenditure or revenue item as controllable or uncontrollable. Such a classification must be made within a specific framework of responsibility and time. For example, the expenses of a particular department would normally include some items such as supervisory salaries that are not ordinarily controllable within the department but that are controllable by higher management. Similarly, certain expenses, such as depreciation, are generally not controllable within the short run but are definitely controllable in the long run. Note that the classifications controllable and fixed or noncontrollable and variable are not synonymous. Generally, in the short run, fixed costs are not subject to the same degree of control as variable costs. Practically all variable costs, by their very nature, are controllable in the short run. Nevertheless, depreciation computed on an output basis is a variable cost but not controllable in the short run. Conversely, certain salaries are controllable yet are fixed costs in the short run.

The concept of responsibility and controllability reporting revolves around the department head and the cost center. Under this concept the man is expected to be concerned with *his* job, *his* initiative, *his* actions, *his* rewards, *his* incentives; therefore, the appropriate accounting should concern itself with *his* sphere of responsibility.

The responsibility cost concept contemplates the dissemination of facts concerning revenues, costs, and investments attributable to the one segment of the company being reported upon. It communicates information about those costs that can be controlled by a person in charge of a specific department. The system should avoid the allocation of costs (for control purposes) to an organizational unit that does not control them and that therefore should not be held responsible for them. Such a reporting system should also follow the organization chart.

The first procedure in initiating a system of responsibility and controllability reporting is the identification of the areas of responsibility and the lines of authority. Each block in the organization chart should represent a segment to be reported upon. Each segment should receive reports on those functions over which it is held responsible. In theory, any report prepared according to this concept fits into one of the blocks in the organization chart. A sample organization chart is shown in Figure 18.1.

The president of the company, who has responsibility for the entire business, would receive an overall expense summary (item D in Figure 18.2) designating the divisions incurring the expenses. At the same time, more specific information on the expenses would be reported to the individual responsible for each division. A very simplified example is given in Figure 18.2. This figure reflects the expense performance compared to budget for each responsibility area and then for an operative subordinate

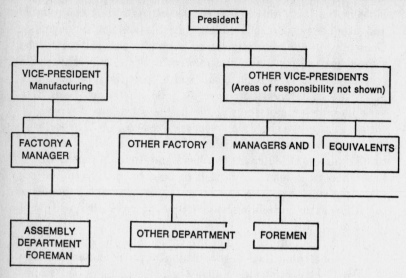

Figure 18.1. Snygen Corporation organization chart

to that area of responsibility. Following this principle of reporting, each person accountable to the president would receive a summary report on the performance of his division along with whatever supporting schedules might be necessary. In Figure 18.2, the vice-president of manufacturing receives an expense performance report matching the responsibility areas of his division (item C in Figure 18.2).

Continuing down the line of authority shown in the organization chart, the factory manager receives a statement of expense performance for each responsibility area reporting to him. Item B of Figure 18.2 shows the expense story of the factory manager's areas of responsibility. The foreman in charge of a department gets his summary as shown in item A.

Under this system of reporting, costs should be compared to the budget by responsibility area. Cumulative costs for the year to date may be far more significant than the results of any one month and should also be shown.

Criteria for a Control System. A glance at Figures 18.1 and 18.2 should indicate that more than a mere accumulation of numbers is needed to make a responsibility accounting system useful. A

SNYGEN CORPORATION

[A] ASSEMBLY DEPARTMENT EXPENSE SUMMARY

ACCOUNT	MONTH		Year to Date	
	Amount	*Over (Under)* *Budget*	Amount	*Over (Under)* *Budget*
Materials	$ 90,000	$(12,000)	$345,000	$ (9,000)
Direct Labor	17,000	(1,000)	68,000	3,000
Indirect Labor	4,000	600	17,000	1,000
Maintenance	25,000	2,000	87,000	(12,000)
All other (itemized)	28,000	3,200	83,000	7,800
→ TOTAL	$164,000	$(7,200)	$600,000	$ (9,200)

[B] FACTORY A EXPENSE SUMMARY

COST CENTER	MONTH		Year to Date	
	Amount	*Over (Under)* *Budget*	Amount	*Over (Under)* *Budget*
↳ [A] Assembly Dept.	$164,000	$(7,200)	$ 600,000	$ (9,200)
Finishing Dept.	87,000	9,600	297,000	(12,000)
All other (itemized) Depts.	249,000	17,200	973,000	19,200
→ TOTAL	$500,000	$ 19,600	$1,870,000	$ (2,000)

[C] MANUFACTURING DIVISION EXPENSE SUMMARY

FACTORY	MONTH		Year to Date	
	Amount	*Over (Under)* *Budget*	Amount	*Over (Under)* *Budget*
↳ [B] Factory A	$ 500,000	$ 19,600	$1,870,000	$ (2,000)
All other (itemized) Depts.	1,300,000	(17,000)	6,420,000	(11,000)
→ TOTAL	$1,800,000	$ 2,600	$8,290,000	$(13,000)

[D] COMPANY EXPENSE SUMMARY

DIVISION	MONTH		Year to Date	
	Amount	*Over (Under)* *Budget*	Amount	*Over (Under)* *Budget*
Central Office	$ 80,000	$ 4,000	$ 360,000	$ (16,000)
↳ [C] Manufacturing	1,800,000	2,600	8,290,000	(13,000)
All other (itemized)	3,420,000	27,400	17,450,000	(143,000)
TOTAL	$5,300,000	$ 34,000	$26,100,000	$(172,000)

Figure 18.2. Flow of responsibility reporting

drawback to the widespread effective use of responsibility accounting is the fact that many firms have designed their cost reporting primarily to obtain historical cost information, largely ignoring the very important matter of controlling costs. Historical costs do provide several kinds of information necessary for control, such as overall operating results, unit costs for pricing inventories, and other cost data necessary for determining prices. However, these are not enough for effective control. The success of a control system depends on additional fundamental concepts that must be applied in order to achieve the results for which the system was designed. These fundamentals are (1) fixing the responsibility for control, (2) measuring the performance of control, and (3) limiting the control effort to controllable costs.

To be effective a control system must have a reasonably accurate method of reporting overall performance and a standard by which to measure actual performance. The standard against which performance is measured is, of course, the budget and all its ramifications in terms of standard and direct costs.

STANDARD OF MEASUREMENT. It is seldom easy to set up a standard of measurement to evaluate executives. The major criterion for the selection of such an index must be one that encompasses as many operating variables as possible. As one progresses up the hierarchy of the organization, it becomes more and more difficult to find one index that encompasses all the variables. At lower levels, perhaps in a production operation, cost could be used as an evaluation index. Of course, concern would center on controllable costs. However, with higher levels in the organization (perhaps at a divisional level), cost will not, by itself, be broad enough to evaluate operations. The evaluation of divisional operations might well require a broader base, such as profits. While profits are a broader index than cost since profits include revenues, profits alone may not be broad enough because of another major variable which must be considered, investment. For example, one division might report a profit of $100,000; another division, a profit of $150,000. It would appear that the second division had done a better job; however, if the first has an investment of $100,000 and the second an investment of $500,000, some question should be raised as to which division is more efficient.

Another method of evaluation is to compare departmental operations against budgets. Once the company determines what actually occurred, it can compare reality against some standard (using standard costs or revenues or whatever other standards may be meaningful) to produce variance information that can be used as the basis for corrective action by higher management. Therefore, once an index of performance is selected, it is necessary to settle on some standard against which actual performance can be compared.

INDEX OF PERFORMANCE. There are many indexes that can be used to evaluate performance. The choice of which index to choose is not a simple one.

Profit Indexes. There are a number of profit indexes that can be used in establishing an index of performance. The four methods discussed here are net profit, direct profit, controllable profit, and contribution margin.

To illustrate these various concepts, we shall use the following profit and loss data for a particular division:

DIVISION X

Division sales revenue	$30,000
Direct division costs:	
Variable costs (all controllable)	21,000
Division controllable fixed overhead	3,000
Division noncontrollable fixed overhead	2,000
Indirect division costs:	
Allocated Fixed Costs	2,000

Several different profit calculations can be developed using the above data. In Figure 18.3, four of the commonly suggested alternatives are presented. These four alternatives are the most reasonable and the most widely used. The names assigned to each are descriptive of the calculation, but there is no standard terminology. The important thing here is to recognize what is included and excluded in each calculation.

NET PROFIT. Many accountants would argue that the most reliable profit measurement to use in measuring division performance is *net profit*. However, net profit is usually calculated after deduction of some share of home office overhead, such as the cost of operating the president's office. The main argument for using net profit is that it makes the division manager aware

	Division Net Profit (1)	Division Direct Profit (2)	Division Controllable Profits (3)	Division Contribution Margin (4)
Revenue	$30,000	$30,000	$30,000	$30,000
Direct cost				
Variable cost	$21,000	$21,000	$21,000	$21,000
				$ 9,000
Controllable fixed cost	3,000	3,000	3,000	
			$ 6,000	
Noncontrollable fixed cost	2,000	2,000		
		$ 4,000		
Indirect allocated fixed costs	2,000			
	$ 2,000			

Figure 18.3. Different profit concepts and measurements

of the full cost of operating his division, even though part of the full cost may not be within his control.

Other accountants feel that the best way to motivate a division manager is to assign only controllable costs to that division and then establish a very rigorous standard of performance. If the manager can be so motivated, he will be concerned only with those costs he can control.

DIRECT PROFIT. Under this method, front office costs are not arbitrarily allocated to the division manager. However, as Figure 18.3 illustrates, some noncontrollable direct costs are usually included in the calculation. Again, if divisional management is to be properly motivated, their efforts should be concentrated only on the costs they can control.

CONTROLLABLE PROFITS. *Controllable profits* are defined as total division revenue in excess of controllable costs. It would seem that for performance measurement this calculation is highly desirable because it concentrates strictly on the cost controllable by division management. If a valid standard is used for comparison, any variance between actual and standard performance can be explained strictly in terms of factors over which the division management has control and responsibility. In the example in Figure 18.3, it is assumed for the sake of simplicity that all variable costs are controllable. However, some noncontrollable but variable costs may be present, for example, depreciation computed on an output basis. Such noncontrollable variable costs would also be excluded in determining the direct division profit.

As an aside, just because a cost is designated as fixed does not mean that the cost is fixed in amount; it may mean fixed in respect to changes in volume. Perhaps the division manager can reduce a fixed cost such as supervisory salaries by reducing the number of supervisors regardless of the level of operation. If this should occur, the new level of costs would still be fixed with respect to volume changes, but because total costs were less, profits would be increased. The point here is that the level of fixed costs can be controlled, and if it is, the division manager should be held responsible for controlling it.

CONTRIBUTION MARGIN. *Contribution margin* is an extremely useful concept in decision making. However, it has some obvious defects if used to evaluate performance. A major one is that controllable items of fixed costs are excluded from calculation, and noncontrollable items of variable costs may be included. If management is to be motivated to perform a specific function, then the information it needs should not be hidden behind items over which it has no control.

While this chapter obviously indicates a preference for the use of controllable profits as the measuring point for evaluating division management, there are some problems in using this index. For example, a division manager may decide to increase his short-run profit at the expense of long-run profit by deferring certain maintenance and repair items. While this will reduce maintenance and repair expense in the short run, it may precipitate a major breakdown.

There are other accounting problems in using controllable profit as an evaluation index, for example, the wide choice of accounting techniques available for computing depreciation or inventories. However, company executives should be able to make allowances for these differences.

The Investment Part of the Index. The last few sections of this chapter have been concerned with the numerator portion of the valuation equation. The next section is concerned with the denominator, investments. If operating divisions are to be evaluated on the basis of rate of return on investments, the proper investment base to be used must be determined. There are many problems and questions connected with the choice of the investment base. The first problem faced is what assets to assign to the division. In an oil refinery that also produces chemicals, there are many processes common to both functions. For example, finished oil products and finished chemical products are processed in the same stills from the same crude oil and then may be shipped through the same pipelines. To which function should the crude oil, stills, and pipelines be charged? On the other hand, many assets can be traced directly to the appropriate division. For example, the division may have its own accounts receivable, its own inventory, and its own cash. There is very little problem dealing with direct investment; the problems occur with joint investment.

Where joint investment is present, arbitrary methods must be used to allocate costs of investments to the various divisions. Since the basis of allocation is necessarily arbitrary, the division managers may have some complaint about the allocation. If the investment index is to be consistent with earlier comments on the allocation of profits and costs (i.e., that the costs to use in determining the profits of a particular division should be those that are controllable only by the division management), then the same criteria should be applied to the investment function. In such a case it might be better not to attempt to allocate common investment. Traceable investment alone would be a better measure of controllable investment than traceable investment plus an allocated share of common investment.

GROSS OR NET PLANT INVESTMENT. Once the business determines which asset should be assigned to which division it must decide whether these assets will be carried at original cost (gross investment) or at original cost less depreciation (net investment). Probably the best justification for the use of gross plant assets in the calculation of divisional rates of return on investment is that it prevents the rate of return from rising as the net book value of depreciable assets is reduced by depreciation. Another argument in support of the use of gross plant assets is that if divisions used different depreciation methods, the impact of these different methods would be washed out of the investment denominator, making interdivisional comparisons more effective. (The use of the different depreciation methods will still affect the numerator.) The proponents of the net asset value basis maintain that it is better because it is consistent with the total assets shown on the conventional balance sheet and with the net income computation, which includes deductions for depreciation.

REPLACEMENT COST. The next problem is probably as significant as the first two. Should the company use historical costs or replacement costs to measure plant assets? For internal purposes it is not required to adhere to conventional accounting practices. Replacement value is probably the best measure because it is the best approximation of current economic sacrifice. However, unless an active market in plant and equipment exists, it is difficult to determine the current replacement values of most plant assets. Because of the complexity and subjectivity involved in obtaining an appraisal value for fixed assets that have no market (as seems to be the case for most corporate fixed assets), the replacement cost method is not favorably regarded.

MEASURING DIVISIONAL PROFITABILITY

As mentioned earlier, where it is possible to allocate revenues, costs, and investments it is feasible to determine both profits and the rate of return of individual product lines, divisions, or departments. In doing so, each division is treated as an autonomous unit with its own return on investment goal. The allocation of investments to the lower levels of a company, for example, to a production department within a factory, could lead to more problems than it would solve. This is particularly true when a substantial number of assets used by that low-level department are the type over which the department has little or no control. In a "good" scheme, a low-level department might be held responsible merely for costs; a higher level department, for costs and revenues; and a factory or division, for investments as well as costs and revenues. In order to allocate costs to a department, division, or product, it is necessary to develop some factor on which overhead can be allocated. There are many methods of allocation.

All departments or divisions of a business affect profit either directly or indirectly. There are some divisions that exist primarily to provide revenues. On the other hand, there are divisions that serve as service departments for the revenue-producing departments. For the purpose of cost analysis, a distinction between these two types of functions and their costs should be made.

Direct-service costs are those incurred by and charged directly to direct-service or revenue-producing departments. *Indirect-service costs* are those incurred by and charged directly to indirect-service or non-revenue-producing departments or sections, such as maintenance, personnel, and general administration. There are many methods of allocating the costs of indirect-service departments to direct-service departments. Some of these are discussed briefly below.

DIRECT ALLOCATION OF OVERHEAD. Under the direct-allocation method, all costs of non-revenue-producing departments are allocated directly to revenue-producing departments. To see how this works, imagine a company that has three revenue-producing departments serviced by one maintenance department. Assume that company management feels that floor space is a good indication of the amount of maintenance time spent on a division. Further assume that Division A has 20 percent of the floor space; Division B, 50 percent of the floor space; and Division C, 30 percent of the floor space. All the maintenance-department costs would be allocated to those three departments on the basis of 20 percent, 50 percent, and 30 percent, respectively. Even though maintenance effort was spent in the administrative department, none of the maintenance charges would be allocated to the administrative function because it is not generally revenue producing. The cost of the administrative function would be allocated to the three divisions on some appropriate basis.

STEP-DOWN METHOD OF ALLOCATING OVERHEAD. The step-down

method is more sophisticated than the direct-allocation method and is a more realistic disposition of the costs of the non-revenue-producing departments. Under the step-down method all costs of non-revenue-producing departments are allocated to all the departments that they serve, whether or not they produce revenues. As the cost of each non-revenue-producing function is allocated in turn, the costing process for that department is considered closed. No further charges are made to that department, and no further allocations are made from it. With this method, the maintenance department expense in the previous example would be allocated to other non-revenue-producing departments as well as to the three producing departments. When the step-down method of cost allocation is used, the section that renders service to the greatest number of other departments is normally allocated first. As a general guideline, when sections render service to an equal number of departments and receive benefits from an equal number of departments, the department that has the greatest amount of expense should be allocated first.

When a non-revenue-producing department is analyzed by this method, its costs are allocated to all other unclosed departments, both revenue- and non-revenue-producing. After all non-revenue-producing departments are closed, all costs will be allocated to the revenue-producing departments. These fully allocated costs are then useful as a basis for pricing services. It follows that all departmental expenses must be presented and carefully analyzed, the direct expenses of each department and the total dollar amount that must be allocated being taken directly from the books of the company.

OTHER METHODS OF ALLOCATING OVERHEAD. In addition to the two methods just discussed, there are many other methods of allocating overhead from one department to another. Some of these methods would be revenue based, which is a form of the direct-allocation method in which expenses of departments are allocated to the revenue-producing departments on some proportion to their revenue.

A double-distribution method is frequently used. Under this method the preliminary allocation of costs of non-revenue-producing departments is made to all departments in an attempt to measure the cost of the services that each of the non-revenue-producing departments renders to the others. This is followed by a financial apportionment of allocating all costs remaining in the non-revenue-producing functions directly to revenue-producing sections.

There is a third, more sophisticated method that is the logical extension of the step-down and double-distribution methods. This method calls for all costs to be distributed to all departments on the basis of a series of simultaneous equations; it ends up allocating all non-revenue-producing costs to all revenue-producing departments. This method has been used by many oil companies.

All the overhead allocation methods mentioned above are described and illustrated in more detail in chapter 8.

TRANSFER PRICING

Intracompany transfers of goods or services create problems in the determination of the profitability of any particular division because the price at which goods or services are transferred represents cost to the buying division and revenue to the selling division. Since both revenues and costs are necessary for the calculation of profit, division heads frequently are in disagreement over internal transfer prices.

These disagreements are part of the reason why there is some opposition to the use of divisional breakdowns for return on investment. The users of divisional measurements have to determine, sometimes arbitrarily, the responsibility for revenues, costs, and investments. Those who disagree with the use of divisional return on investment measures maintain that comparisons against standards or budgets are both more meaningful and less counterproductive than divisional return on investment and avoid the entire hassle of determining division costs, profits, and investments.

In recording intracompany transfers, there are several possible transfer prices. The four that will be discussed in this section are full historical cost, direct cost, market price, and negotiated price.

Full Cost. Transfer prices based on cost are very commonly used. They are also difficult to justify as a measure for performance evaluation except as a matter of convenience. Because no intermediate market exists, some companies have no other choice but to use prices based on cost. In such cases, many use full cost alone or full cost plus some profit allowance for this purpose.

The objection to using full cost as the basis for setting transfer prices arises from the fact that there is no reason for the intermediate seller to control costs; he will recover them all on sale. If internal costs are not compared to external costs, inefficiencies will be more difficult to detect.

Direct Cost. The use of direct costs to establish transfer prices from one division to another within a company leads to similar problems. While transfer prices based on direct costs may lead to efficient short-run use of firm assets, there are some psychological problems, particularly where controllable fixed costs are involved. When outside markets exist for the product at an intermediate stage of production, it may be better, given the proper cost and revenue situations, for the company to sell the product rather than complete it. The information necessary to arrive at a correct decision under such circumstances is frequently unavailable with the use of direct costs only.

Market Price. Some companies use market prices as the ceiling for transfer prices in interdivisional transfers. A transfer price system based on the market would set greater reliance on open market transactions than on internal costs. The usefulness of any such system is limited by the availability of market information. Where there is no market, there can be no market price system. Where an open market exists, this system has great validity for the evaluation of performance.

Negotiated Prices. The market price transfer system sets a ceiling, the market price, for interdivision transfers. However, there are many instances where savings may be incurred because of larger purchases, lower selling costs, exclusive supplier contracts, or other advantages for intracompany dealings. In such cases, negotiations that will lower the market price charged one division by another may take place between the division managers. This process is known as negotiated market pricing. Market prices are also likely to be negotiated when there is no market for the intermediate product being transferred.

The big drawback in negotiated market prices is that when there is a dispute between equal-ranking division managers, someone must settle that dispute.

CHAPTER 19

Statistical Methods and Operations Research

No book on cost accounting is complete without at least a brief discussion of the applications of statistics and operations research to cost accounting problems. This chapter will show how certain of these quantitative techniques can be useful to the modern cost accountant.

COST ACCOUNTING AND STATISTICS

Statistical sampling, statistical quality control, control charts, and probability analysis have been advantageously applied to a number of cost accounting problems.

Statistical Sampling. Statistics is defined as "a branch of mathematics dealing with the collection, analysis, interpretation, and presentation of masses of numerical data."[1] The most common application of the statistician's art is in sampling. In statistics, all the data available on a subject are called a population or a universe. Sampling is the technique of counting only a portion of that universe under the assumption that the sample will represent the universe. The usefulness of this technique is demonstrated in the political field. Pollsters are sometimes wrong but usually only when they have predicted a close election. Predictions derived from sampling are frequently used in manufacturing as the basis for quality control. Sampling is also adaptable to many areas of accounting, including cost accounting.

The validity of sampling techniques is sometimes questioned

[1] *Webster's Seventh New Collegiate Dictionary* (Springfield, Mass.: G & C Merriam Company, 1963).

from the standpoint that nothing less than a 100 percent count can be accurate. But in many cases it is impossible to get an accurate 100 percent count. Try counting the beans in a jar or the washers in a storage bin. If, however, we find that 13 washers weigh one pound, we can be pretty sure that 97.5 pounds of washers would count out to 1267+ washers. Even if the actual count (assuming we could find people who would make no errors in such a tedious job) were 1265 or 1270, it would make no practical difference. But the cost of hiring people to do the counting would make a great deal of difference.

There are limitations to the use of statistical sampling. Any sampling technique requires a reasonable number of observations before a high degree of statistical significance can be read from the results. While it may be possible to obtain a reasonable number of observations based on past data, such data may not be relevant to future events.

The discussions in chapters 11 and 13 regarding the breakdown of the variable and fixed portions of expense involved the use of a regression analysis, which is an application of a form of statistical sampling and analysis. The warnings in those chapters concerning the relevant range are applicable to statistical sampling in other forms, too. If a curve is being fitted to a group of observations in a particular range, it is not necessarily true that the same curve will apply to observations falling outside that range. In fact, it would be very surprising if this were the case.

Statistical Quality Control. For many years industry has used certain statistical techniques to control the physical characteristics of production processes. Under some conditions these statistical techniques may also be used to control the costs of the production process. Typically, statistical quality control is based on the analysis of variance from a standard that is based on some expected mean value. Because the mean value of the standard is rarely known for most manufacturers, an estimate of that mean might be based on samples of the actual process.

For purposes of statistical quality control, the standard is expressed as a range or confidence interval based on the mean value of the standard and some estimate of its variability. Within that range or confidence interval, performance is acceptable.

If there are observations outside that range, or if there are a series of observations trending toward one of the outer limits of the interval, the production process is considered to be out of control. If the process is out of control, it will probably be most economical to attempt to bring the process back into control.

Control Charts. In some cases, it may be useful to prepare what is called a *control chart* to determine the variability of the process. This is done because the mean may remain under control but the variability of the process may increase, particularly where less skilled workers are employed in the process or new machines are being broken in.

The use of the control chart is an aid in determining which of those observations that deviate from the standard are random and which indicate situations that need further investigation. If the deviation is merely random, it need not be investigated. Identification of the random deviation thus will save both the cost of investigation and the production costs that might result from overcompensating for such deviations.

The sample control chart in Figure 19.1 is designed to show whether the company is using an acceptable level of materials in its production process. Observations 9, 11, and 14 fall outside the accepted range of material per unit. In these samples 9, 8½, and 3 pounds of material per unit, respectively, are used. As soon as these conditions appeared, management was alerted to the fact that the production process was probably out of control; steps were taken to investigate causes; and corrections were made. Correction does not mean that the production process is improved; it merely means that the output or outcome of the

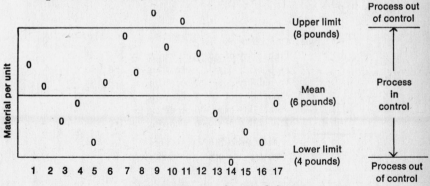

Figure 19.1. Sample control chart

production process is more predictable. In employing this type of chart, management has a practical method of determining which variations from the standard are significant. Note that of all the observations taken, none was directly on the mean.

Probability Analysis. Many, if not most, businesses operate under circumstances in which future events cannot be predicted with any degree of certainty. If any businessman operated in a world of certainty, his only excuse for making a wrong decision would be the failure to account for some particular factor. This is so because certainty is defined statistically as the ability to make a perfect forecast of all relevant factors. However, when all of the relevant facts are not known, management is forced to gamble that a particular set of facts will exist, hence decisions are at best optimum.

The absence of knowledge about all relevant facts is known as uncertainty, the presence of which necessitates a reliance on probability analysis. Under conditions involving probability analysis, recognition is made that several possible alternative events may occur. Frequently, the probability of an occurrence can be objectively determined. For example, given the rolling of an honest die with six sides, the probability of each side occurring is exactly 1/6. The total probabilities of some side appearing can be mathematically added to equal one. This is always true of probabilities; when all possible events are listed, the listing is done in such a way that no two events can happen at the same time, and when all possible events are listed, the total chances of all occurrences are equal to one. This is demonstrated in Figure 19.2.

Given: One roll of one die:
    Probability of side 1 occurring $= 1/6$
    Probability of side 2 occurring $= 1/6$
    Probability of side 3 occurring $= 1/6$
    Probability of side 4 occurring $= 1/6$
    Probability of side 5 occurring $= 1/6$
    Probability of side 6 occurring $= 1/6$
                    —
    Total probability of one of
     all possible events occurring $= 1$

Figure 19.2. Probability of occurrence

The probability of side 6 occurring on the roll of the die is objective in the sense that it can be and has been verified through many historical trials. In many business decisions it is possible to assign objective probabilities to specific outcomes because there is much historical experience available. These probabilities are called objective because there is available information on which the probability is based. This would be particularly true in a repetitive-type production process.

SUBJECTIVE PROBABILITIES. All too frequently, however, there is just not enough objective information available about a given situation to enable a businessman to ascertain the probability of a particular outcome. When the outcomes are unmeasurable, there are two ways in which a businessman can approach a problem. The first is to use intuitive judgment and hunches without evaluating; the second is to evaluate the intuitive judgments and use those intuitive judgments to supply subjective probabilities. Most problems of uncertainty can be handled by assigning subjective probabilities to possible events and then proceeding to a solution via the mathematical theory of probability.

As a practical matter, the use of probability theory can help a businessman or accountant explicitly determine the degree of uncertainty in any cost accounting problem and can put a price on that uncertainty. If it is possible to seek additional information and the cost of seeking that additional information is less than the cost of uncertainty, it would pay to seek additional information. On the other hand, if the cost of seeking additional information exceeds the cost of uncertainty, it does not pay to seek additional information but rather to act on the best possible outcome predicted with the information on hand.

PAYOFF TABLE. Traditionally, probability analysis is an approach whereby each of the possible outcomes of a specific decision is assigned a value and the probability of each outcome occurring is assigned a weight. The value of each outcome is then multiplied by the weighted probability of its occurring, and the resulting products of all of the values are added to determine the expected value of the given decision.

In order to illustrate the building and use of payoff tables, a simple business situation involving the use of probability theory follows.

A bakery bakes fresh loaves of bread daily. These loaves cost $.15 each to bake, slice, and wrap. The bread sells for $.30 a loaf. Any loaves left over at the end of the day are sold to a nearby pig farm for use as feed at $.14 each. The daily demand for fresh bread ($.30 loaves) is estimated as follows:

Demand in loaves	Probability of occurrence
200	.20
250	.20
300	.30
350	.20
400	.10
Total probability	1.00

The baker's problem is to determine how many loaves he must produce in order to maximize profits. The profit per loaf sold as fresh bread is $.15, and the loss per loaf sold as feed is $.01. All alternatives are assessed below in Figure 19.3 in the form of a payoff table.

Most business decisions may be made using the expected-monetary-value approach indicated in Figure 19.3. In other words, business managers will make a decision that brings the greatest financial advantage to the business. However, there are very many situations where this will not be true, particularly where the chance of loss is great relative to the assets of the business. Where stakes are very large, the dollar of profit available may be worth less to the business than the risk of a dollar of loss. In such cases, the utility value of the dollars of profits or losses must be examined in relationship to the business. When this situation is present, the decision-making approach is the same as illustrated in Figure 19.3, but instead of using dollar values the businessman would use utility values. Utility values are direct expressions of the personal preferences or risk avoidance characteristics of the particular businessman.

A look at Figure 19.3 shows us that even though 90 percent of the time the bakery will sell less than 400 loaves as fresh bread, it would still pay to produce 400 loaves because the expected value is higher than that of any other alternative. Note, however, that if the feed loaves could be sold for only $.10 each, instead of

Event: Demand for fresh loaves	Probability of event	Act: Fresh loaves baked 200		250		300		350		400	
		C.V.*	E.V.†	C.V.	E.V.	C.V.	E.V.	C.V.	E.V.	C.V.	E.V.
200	.20	$30.00	$ 6.00	$29.50	$ 5.90	$29.00	$ 5.80	$28.50	$ 5.70	$28.00	$ 5.60
250	.20	30.00	6.00	37.50	7.50	37.00	7.40	36.50	7.30	36.00	7.20
300	.30	30.00	9.00	37.50	11.25	45.00	13.50	44.50	13.35	44.00	13.20
350	.20	30.00	6.00	37.50	7.50	45.00	9.00	52.50	10.50	52.00	10.40
400	.10	30.00	3.00	37.50	3.75	45.00	4.50	52.50	5.25	60.00	6.00
Total expected value			$30.00		$35.90		$40.20		$42.10		$42.40

*Conditional value: The conditional value is the profit from that specific event occurring. The conditional value is computed as [Fresh loaves sold × ($.30−$.15) + feed loaves sold × ($.14−$.15)].
† Expected value: The expected value is the conditional value × the probability of such a condition occurring.

Figure 19.3. Bakery payoff table

$.14, the best level of operations for that bakery would be only 350 loaves a day as expected profits would be maximized at $39.50.

MATHEMATICAL MODELS IN OPERATIONS RESEARCH

The idea underlying operations research is the assumption that the problems facing business can be reduced to a mathematical model that can be used to evaluate alternatives for future strategy. This mathematical model is a statement of relationships between the important factors in the real situation. The model is an abstraction because most real-life situations are too complex to be fully stated mathematically with any meaning.

With operations research, management or accountants express the business situation in the form of mathematical equations and/or inequalities. The more complex the situation, the more complex the mathematical model. For most business situations, the mathematical model, the number of equations, and the type of mathematics necessary to solve the models require the use of digital computers.

Because mathematical models are only abstractions, they cannot be truly representative. However, to be useful, they must be representative of actual relationships. Businessmen will sometimes use a model that is unrealistic or will apply a model designed for one purpose to an entirely different situation. In cases such as this, the fault lies not with the model but with the user.

Applications of Operations Research to Accounting. Operations research tools are used in solving many of the problems with which the accountant must grapple. One of these problems involves the relation of one inventory component to another. Where a complex assembly requires a large number of parts in varying quantities with a staggered time sequence of availability, we have what is called a *queuing* or *probability problem.* Queuing theory has been applied to the determination of how many lines to have open at a cafeteria, how many attendants to have at a service station, and so on.

Another kind of problem in which operations research techniques can be used is the case where two factors are partially independent of and partially dependent on each other. A good example of this is the interrelationship of the classical economic supply and demand curves. The formulation covering this situation is called a *correlation model*. Still another problem that can be dealt with by operations research techniques is the best use of scarce resources, for example, the bakery problem illustrated in Figure 19.3. The problem can be reduced to a formula that, with relevant data, can be programmed into a computer or solved manually. One resource, cash, is by definition always a scarce resource. This reduction to a formula of the problem of resource optimization is called *linear programming*.

To illustrate how linear programming might be used, a simple linear-programming problem and its solution, both graphically and mathematically, is given below. (For larger problems, electronic computers and the simplex method must be used. However, even for the largest of problems, mechanical solutions are not nearly as difficult as the determination of the problem and the relevant economic data. This is so because linear programming is merely a set of simultaneous linear equations representing the model of the problem.)

The Andersen Company produces two products, A and B. Information regarding the products is presented below in Figure 19.4.

	Product A	Product B
Sales price per unit	$11.00	$ 9.00
Variable cost per unit	5.00	4.00
Contribution margin per unit	$ 6.00	$ 5.00
Production time in hours	4	2
Estimated demand in units	30,000	80,000
Total production time available	200,000 hours	

Figure 19.4. Linear programming data

In common with all linear-programming problems, Andersen wishes to maximize its quantity or contribution margin. In order to do this, it must know how many units of each product to produce and sell. The contribution margin of Product A is $6; that of Product B, $5. There are two marketing constraints and one production constraint. Mathematically, this problem can be expressed as:

Maximize: Contribution margin = $6 A + $5 B
Subject to: 4A and 2B = 200,000 (production constraint)
            A =   30,000 (market constraint on A)
            B =   80,000 (market constraint on B)

It is possible to solve this set of equations using algebra. The problem requires a simultaneous solution to four equations, and such a solution consists of finding values for A and B that will result in an objective function (contribution margin) as large as possible but that does not violate any constraint. This solution turns out to be 10,000 units of A and 80,000 units of B. At this sales mix, the contribution margin is $460,000 and violates neither market nor production constraints.

With only two products, regardless of the number of constraints, this problem could have been solved graphically as illustrated in Figure 19.5.

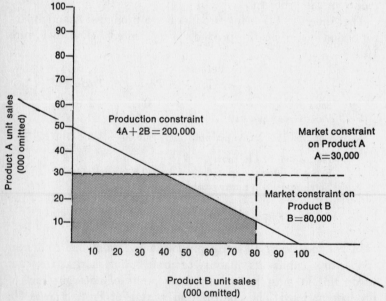

Figure 19.5. Graphic solution to linear-programming problem

The shaded portion of Figure 19.5 has five corner points. Note that the graphic technique will handle almost any number of restraints; however, it will handle only two products. If more than two products are involved, the graph requires more than two dimensions and therefore becomes much more difficult to work with.

For such situations a generalized algebraic solution, the simplex method, is available for solving linear-programming problems.

Returning to Figure 19.5, there are three constraints used in the example. In this problem, as in any two-dimensional, linear-programming problem, the optimal solution is found on a boundary formed by the constraints, as illustrated in Figure 19.6.

Corner	Combination A *(units)*	B *(units)*	Total contribution margin
0,0	0	0	($6)(0) +($5)(0) =$ 0
30,0	30,000	0	($6)(30,000)+($5)(0) =$180,000
30,40	30,000	40,000	($6)(30,000)+($5)(40,000)=$380,000
10,80	10,000	80,000	($6)(10,000)+($5)(80,000)=$460,000*
0,80	0	80,000	($6)(0) +($5)(80,000)=$400,000

* Optimum solution

Figure 19.6. Using corner points to determine optimum sales

Eventually, the simplex method checks out each corner point, stopping at that product combination yielding the highest contribution margin. In this example, A = 10,000, B = 80,000, yields the highest contribution margin, or $460,000.

As demonstrated above, linear-programming techniques can be used to solve problems involving product combinations. The techniques can also be used to minimize production costs or maximize product quality. The real impact of linear programming, however, is not so much what it can do for the cost accountant, but what the cost accountant can do for the management that uses linear programming. Most of the data called for by linear programming are provided by the cost accountant: the concepts of variable costs, contribution margin, and rate of return per scarce factor. In a real sense, linear programming improves upon and is an extension of the accounting technique of cost-volume-profit analysis.

Problems

2.1. The Handy Dandy Cornflake Company makes one product in one factory. The company is considering expanding its manufacturing facility and cannot decide whether to double the size of its present factory or to acquire another plant site some distance away.

Handy Dandy currently produces 100,000 units with a total variable cost of $75,000 and a total fixed cost of $100,000. If the company doubles the size of its current plant, total variable costs will rise proportionately, but fixed costs will become $205,000. If the company buys a new factory to produce 200,000 units, total fixed costs will be $178,000, but total variable costs will rise to $180,000.

Required: Determine which alternative the company should choose if it expects to average

- (a) 150,000 units per year in sales
- (b) 180,000 units
- (c) 200,000 units

3.1. My Own Company has made several purchases of a raw material used in a new manufacturing process. During the year, various production runs were completed using some of this material. The information concerning purchases and issues follows:

Purchases:

January 15	200 units @ $3.00/unit	
March 9	600 units @ $3.10/unit	
May 17	400 units @ $3.05/unit	
June 19	500 units @ $3.06/unit	
August 24	700 units @ $3.10/unit	
November 27	400 units @ $3.15/unit	
December 29	400 units @ $3.20/unit	
Total	3,200 units	

Issues:

February 6	100 units
March 28	400 units
April 18	100 units
June 10	300 units
July 26	400 units
September 15	300 units
October 17	500 units
December 15	800 units
Total	2,900 units

Required: Determine the value of the ending inventory using FIFO, periodic LIFO, and weighted-average techniques. There was no beginning inventory.

3.2. The Petite Safe Company plans to use 300,000 sets of 8-inch hinges for the coming year. The cost of placing an order is $15, and the cost of storing 100 sets of hinges for a year is $225.
Required: Determine the economic order quantity.

4.1. Genmik Corporation has the following transactions in the first month of operation:

(1)	Materials purchased	$10,000
(2)	Wages paid—direct labor	8,000
(3)	Salaries (factory supervisor and clerical)	1,300
(4)	Materials issued to departments	4,000
(5)	Materials included in finished goods	3,000
(6)	Direct labor included in finished goods	5,000
(7)	Rent, power, water, etc.	2,500
(8)	Wages paid—indirect labor	2,800

The standard overhead rate is 75% of direct labor.

Required: Prepare T-accounts and a trial balance of the fore-going factory transactions. Cash or accounts payable may be used as a balancing account.

4.2. The Ogden Company manufactures widgets to special order. On July 31, the books of the company showed the following balances:

Raw materials control	$200,000
Work in process control	
Job 17	83,000
Job 18	62,000
Job 19	11,000
Total	$356,000

The following transactions pertaining to Jobs 17, 18, and 19 occurred in August:

(1) Direct labor costs were used on the jobs as follows:

Job 17	3,000 hours @ $4.20/hr.	$12,600
Job 18	4,500 hours @ $4.10/hr.	18,450
Job 19	6,500 hours @ $4.00/hr.	26,000

(2) Materials were requisitioned for the jobs as follows:

Job 17	$12,400
Job 18	11,550
Job 19	27,000

(3) Overhead costs are charged to jobs at the rate of $5 per direct-labor hour.

(4) The jobs were finished and billed to customers. Job 17 was billed at $180,000; Job 18, at $140,000; and Job 19, at $100,000.

Required:

(a) Give the journal entries to summarize each of the August transactions.

(b) Determine the gross profit rate on sales price for each job.

5.1. Gensy Corporation uses the modified FIFO process cost system. Using the following facts:

Units in beginning inventory	25,000 (40% completed)
Units transferred in	100,000
Units transferred out	105,000
Units in closing inventory	20,000 (50% completed)
Value of beginning inventory	$60,000
Costs transferred in:	
Materials	$75,000
Labor and overhead	$60,000
Materials added	$55,000
Labor and overhead added	$136,500

All materials are added at the beginning of the process in this department.

Required:
(a) Compute the equivalent units processed.
(b) Compute the value of the goods transferred out.
(c) Compute the value of the closing inventory.

6.1. Skimik Corporation produces Products A, B, and C from the same basic raw material. Product A had an average selling price last month of $1.25 per unit; Product B, an average selling price of $2 per unit; and Product C, an average selling price of $15 per unit. Three thousand units of A, 2,400 units of B, and 400 units of C were produced from $2,400 of raw materials. It cost $3,000 to process the raw materials to the split-off point. Thereafter, it cost $1,250 to process Product A, $800 to process Product B, and $2,500 to process Product C. There were no beginning or ending inventories of raw materials.

Required: Assign costs to each of the products.

6.2. Geno Corporation processed 11,000 units of raw materials last month for which it paid $60 per unit. For every 11 units of raw materials used, 10 units of output were obtained. During the month Geno Corporation's production took the following mix:

Product	Production percentage	Market price
C	60	$120/unit
D	30	$180/unit
F	10	$ 30/unit

In this time period labor and overhead costs were $200,000, and sales were 5,000 units of C, 2,500 of D, and 1,000 of F.

Required: Using the average market price as your basis,

(a) compute cost of goods manufactured

(b) compute cost of goods sold

(c) compute ending inventory of finished goods.

In all three requirements assume no beginning or ending inventories of work in process and no beginning inventory of finished goods.

7.1. Keerst Company has a manufacturing process under which some production losses occur because of spoilage caused by worker negligence. In the most recent operating period the following production took place:

Beginning inventory	10,000 units
	60% completed
Transferred in	21,000 units
Spoiled production	1,000 units
Transferred out	18,000 units
Ending inventory	12,000 units
	50% completed

The total costs of production, including the value of the beginning inventory, amounted to $48,000. The company uses the weighted-average method of computing equivalent units.

Required: Calculate the unit cost assuming

(a) spoiled production is excluded from the equivalent unit base

(b) spoiled production is included in the equivalent unit base

8.1. The Fad Company is a manufacturing concern. The company is organized into six departments, three service departments and three revenue-producing departments. The service departments are administrative, maintenance, and design; the three revenue-producing departments are consumer products, industrial products, and government services. Pertinent facts for the month of May are:

FAD COMPANY

	Service Departments			Revenue-Producing Departments		
	Adminis-tration (A)	Mainte-nance (M)	Design (D)	Consumer (C)	Industrial (I)	Govern-ment (G)
Overhead costs	$300,000	$180,000	$100,000	$100,000	$150,000	$200,000
Employees	200	100	50	100	100	150
Floor space (square feet)	20,000	9,000	10,000	20,000	30,000	20,000
Design hours	1,000	1,000	0	3,000	4,000	1,000
Direct-labor hours				20,000	40,000	10,000

The company has decided to allocate administration costs on the basis of the number of employees in each department, maintenance costs on the basis of square feet of floor space, and design costs on the basis of design hours worked.

Required:
   (a) Allocate the overhead costs to producing departments using the single-step method.
   (b) Determine the overhead cost per direct labor hour for each revenue-producing department.

8.2. Solve problem 8.1 using multiple equations.

9.1. The Koley Manufacturing Company manufactures its one product from a raw material which it purchases in carload lots of fifty tons each. Material costs last year averaged $400 per ton, and it is anticipated that costs this year will be 5 percent higher. Manufacturing is done at a uniform rate throughout the year using about twenty tons of raw materials each month. The raw materials must be paid for thirty days after receipt. Raw materials are ordered so there will never be less than twenty tons on hand at the end of a month.

Wages, salaries, and all other cash expenditures total $10,000 per month. Depreciation is $1,200 per month. Sales are uneven throughout the year. They are $40,000 per month in January, February, March, and April; $10,000 per month in May, June, July, and August; and $25,000 per month thereafter. As at December 31 of the previous year, there were sufficient inventories of finished products on hand to carry sales through the peak months early in the year. Thirty tons of raw material were on hand, and a carload of raw material was due to be delivered in January. Sales are made on account, and all accounts are paid within sixty days. A line of credit of $100,000 is available at a local bank. A dividend of $20,000 is payable in February. Federal and state income taxes due March 15 are $30,000. Cash on hand January 1 is $30,000. The credit agreement requires a cash balance of at least $25,000 to be on hand at the end of each month.

Required: Prepare a cash budget for the ensuing year.

9.2. The Burgess Company has recently started in business and is interested in installing a flexible budgeting system to strengthen its system of planning and control. They have come to you for advice in setting up such a system and have asked you to help prepare their first budget. In examining the company's records and conversing with some qualified engineers, you determine the cost structure in the manufacturing division.

In this division the following monthly costs are relevant:

Fixed:	
Depreciation	$ 2,000
Rent	8,000
Supervisors	7,000
Total	$17,000
Variable per unit of output:	
Electricity	$ .30
Repairs	.10
Maintenance	.25
Wages	6.00
Materials	2.00
Total	$8.65

Required:
 (a) Construct a budget for 30,000 units of output.
 (b) Construct a budget for 40,000 units of output.

10.1. Given the following facts:

	Budgeted	*Actual*
Fixed overhead	$8,000	$8,350
Variable overhead	$14,000	$15,500
Direct labor hours	4,000	4,200
Units produced	20,000	19,500

Required: Analyze the overhead.

10.2. The Stacey Company produces KES in standard batches of 500 units. Last month's production amounted to 60 batches. The company uses a standard-cost system, and the following data for last month are available:

Overhead cost	$125,000
Raw materials used	30,000 lbs.
Cost of raw materials	$15,000
Direct labor (50,000 hours)	$200,000

The standard costs for producing a batch of KES are:

Overhead	800 hours @ $2.60 per hour	$2,080
Raw materials	550 lbs. @ $ .60 per lb.	330
Direct labor	800 hours @ $4.00 per hour	3,200
		$5,610

Required: Analyze the variances for overhead, labor, and materials. Show all computations.

11.1. Given the following facts:

Units of output: 0–500,000
Fixed costs: $750,000
Variable cost per unit: $2
Selling price per unit: $5

Required: Graph a conventional break-even chart, a preferred break-even chart, and a profit graph.

Prove your answer, using the formulas, to determine the break-even point, the sales needed for a profit of $600,000, and the profit if 400,000 units are sold at $6 per unit.

11.2. The Scharles Company is interested in analyzing its current operations. Investigation shows that for each $100 of sales, variable costs amount to $70, and fixed costs amount to $300,000 per year.

Required:

(a) Compute the break-even point.
(b) If the company has an increase in fixed costs of $60,000, what is the new break-even point?
(c) If variable costs fall to $60 per $100 sales, what will be the break-even point? Disregard part b.
(d) If the company wants to return 15 percent profit on its $200,000 investment, how much must it sell? Ignore parts b and c.

Problem 12.1 is on p. 231.

12.2. Miroz Corporation is a manufacturer of fine widgets for home and industrial use. Its standards of material usage in production for the coming year were set as follows:

$$
\begin{array}{lll}
60 \text{ units of R @ } \$3 = & \$180 \\
20 \text{ units of Q @ } \quad 2 = & 40 \\
20 \text{ units of T @ } \quad 1 = & 20 \\
\hline
\text{Total cost} & \$240 \text{ for 100 widgets or} \\
& \$2.40 \text{ per widget}
\end{array}
$$

The production manager feels that by substituting 30 additional units of T, 15 units of R could be saved. While defective production might increase to 10 percent of total production, the savings in cost would offset this.

Required: Comment on the production manager's plan, showing the impact of the change in material mix on the standards set.

13.1. The Eddy Company manufactures an inexpensive telephone answering and recording device that comes in only one

12.1. The LeMoine Corporation had the following budgets and actual results for the current year:

| | Products | | | | | | | | |
| | A | | | B | | | Totals | | |
	Units	Price	Totals	Units	Price	Totals	Units	Price	Totals
Budget									
Sales	30,000	$6.00	$180,000	50,000	$8.00	$400,000	80,000	$7.25	$580,000
Variable costs	30,000	4.00	120,000	50,000	6.00	300,000	80,000	5.25	420,000
Contribution margin	30,000	$2.00	$ 60,000	50,000	$2.00	$100,000	80,000	$2.00	$160,000
Actual									
Sales	40,000	$6.20	$248,000	50,000	$7.64	$382,000	90,000	$7.00	$630,000
Variable costs	40,000	4.10	164,000	50,000	5.72	286,000	90,000	5.00	450,000
Contribution margin	40,000	$2.10	$ 84,000	50,000	$1.92	$ 96,000	90,000	$2.00	$180,000

Required: As an analyst for the company, determine the causes for the increased profitability.

model. Each device sells for $99. The variable costs of production are $33 per unit, while fixed costs of production total $166,000. All salesmen are salaried, and goods are sold FOB shipping point, hence there are no variable selling costs. Fixed selling costs total $90,000, and fixed administrative costs are $142,000.

Required:
- (a) Determine the contribution margin per unit.
- (b) Prepare a direct-costing income statement for a sales volume of 10,000 units.

14.1. The Choffmann Corporation has an opportunity to manufacture its principal product to be retailed under a proprietary name. This action will probably not affect sales of its own brand because the potential customer is seeking only a replacement for a present source that has discontinued its line. There is ample plant capacity to take on this new production.

Salient facts from Choffmann's operating statement are:

Principal Product Division

Sales	100,000 Units	$10,000,000
Cost of goods sold*		6,500,000
Gross profit		$ 3,500,000
Selling, general, and administrative expense		1,200,000
Contribution margin		$ 2,300,000

* Includes depreciation, $300,000; taxes, insurance, and other fixed costs, $500,000

The customer proposes to buy 40,000 units annually at a price of $70 each.

Required: Determine whether or not the company should take the business.

14.2. The Racquet and Ski Shop has just completed a disastrous ski season. While sales of ski equipment were almost average, sales of ski clothing were way below expectations. As a result, the store has parkas, pants, and sweaters left in stock with a list price of $40,000 and an average markup of 40 percent of selling price.

The company is in somewhat of a cash bind and is faced with two alternatives to raise cash necessary to continue operations.

(1) Wholesale the clothing through a local broker with national connections. The amount to be realized would be 70 percent of cost.

(2) Run a special sale at cost. The advertising expense involved would run $2,000, and management feels that at least 50 percent of what is remaining could be sold. The remainder would be held until the following year when they could be sold at cost less 20 percent as loss leaders.

Required: Assuming that proceeds of the sales would be used to pay bills with average discount terms of 4 percent for prompt payment, which alternative should the company adopt?

15.1. At 6 percent, how long would it take to amortize an investment of $25,000, on which the payback is $2,982 annually?

15.2. What is the rate of return where there is a right to receive $7,142 in 10 years, after an initial investment of $2,000?

15.3. What is the present value of the right to receive $4,000 a year for 8 years, using a 7 percent rate of return?

16.1. The Winkler Candy Company wants to increase its profits by raising prices and instituting an additional advertising campaign. It currently has the following manufacturing and selling costs per 100,000 boxes of candy:

Manufacturing costs:
Direct materials	$100,000 ⎫	
Direct labor	50,000 ⎬ varies in proportion to volume	
Variable overhead	50,000 ⎭	
Selling costs—Variable	35,000 ⎬ varies in proportion to revenues	

Fixed costs are estimated at $100,000 for manufacturing overhead and $200,000 for selling and administrative expenses for the year. Current sales volume is 400,000 boxes at a price of $3.50 per box. The company will increase prices to $3.75 per box but expects sales volume to remain constant as the result of a new advertising campaign.

Required: Determine how much more the company can spend on advertising and still raise profits by 50 percent.

16.2. The Raber Corporation has four retail departments in its store. Sales of products, costs of products, and floor space are as follows:

Product	Sales	Cost of Product	Floor Space (in square feet)
A	$ 75,000	$ 45,000	1,000
B	$125,000	$ 75,000	2,500
C	$ 50,000	$ 25,000	500
D	$100,000	$ 70,000	1,000

Nonassignable costs are $75,000. The usual practice in the trade is to assign costs on a weighted-average basis depending on the varying desirability of display space, the space occupied by A being rated 200; B and C, 150; and D, 100.

Required:
(a) Compute the marginal contribution and assigned costs of each department.
(b) Determine what problems are introduced by the computation of net profits after assigned costs by product.

18.1. The Raber Corporation has three divisions, and the following operating facts are derived from its financial statements:

	Total	A	B	C
Sales	$1,000,000	$ 500,000	$300,000	$200,000
Divisional costs	700,000	400,000	200,000	100,000
Gross profit	300,000	100,000	100,000	100,000
Corporate expense	250,000	125,000	75,000	50,000
Net profit	$ 50,000	$ (25,000)	$ 25,000	$ 50,000
Assets	$ 250,000	$ 50,000	$100,000	$100,000

Required: Analyze the profits of the Raber Corporation.

18.2. F. Sing and Company has two major divisions, D and F. Division D produces a component which is utilized by Division

F in making widgets to sell to the general public. Both the component (nidget) and the final product (widget) have markets outside the company. Because of the existence of external markets, both divisions are considered profit centers by company management. The transfer price for nidgets is set by the company economist based on long-run average market prices.

You are the senior vice-president for F. Sing and Company and are evaluating the following data:

Widget selling price	$400
Nidget selling price	300
Variable cost in Division D	200
Variable cost in Division F	160

Division F always shows losses on production of widgets because its variable costs exceed the additional revenue gained by transferring nidgets to widgets.

Nidget selling price	$300
Variable cost in Division F	160
Total variable cost	$460
Widget selling price	$400

The company can produce up to 20,000 each of nidgets and widgets.

Required:

(a) Determine whether the company should continue the operation of Division F if all nidgets produced can be sold on the open market.

(b) Assume that the company is capable of producing 20,000 nidgets but can only sell 14,000 on the open market. Should the company then continue to produce 6,000 widgets?

19.1. The Smerk Company produces two products and wants to produce the number of units of each product that will enable Smerk to maximize its profit. In developing a response to the company's stated goal, you uncover the following:

	Product A	Product B
Unit sales price	$15.00	$25.00
Unit variable cost	9.00	18.00
Unit contribution margin	$ 6.00	$ 7.00
Production time in hours	1	2
Estimated unit demand	40,000	50,000
Total production time available	120,000 hours	

Required: Determine the maximum contribution margin the Smerk Company can obtain under the given constraints.

19.2. Tax Accountants Incorporated, a firm engaged in preparing individual income tax returns, is concerned with hiring enough help for one of its locations. Most of the people using this firm want immediate service and if not handled promptly will probably go to a competitor or decide to do their own return.

A helper (tax return preparer) is paid $150 per week and can handle twenty tax returns at an average price of $20 apiece. Helpers are paid by contract whether or not there is sufficient demand for their services.

Required: Determine the optimum number of preparers to hire for the coming season (lasting 12 weeks). *Hint:* The best way to go about this is to develop a payoff table from the following assumptions:

Expected number of returns to process	Number of preparers required to process	Probability of each event occurring
960	4	.20
1,200	5	.40
1,440	6	.30
1,680	7	.10
		1.00

Answers

2.1. (a) At 150,000 units expansion would cost

Fixed costs	$205,000
Variable cost $\dfrac{\$150,000}{200,000 \text{ units}} \times 150,000 \text{ units} =$	112,500
Total cost	$317,500

The new plant would cost

Fixed costs	$178,000
Variable cost $\dfrac{\$180,000}{200,000 \text{ units}} \times 150,000 \text{ units} =$	135,000
Total cost	$313,000

Therefore, at 150,000 units the company should buy the new factory.

(b) At 180,000 units expansion costs would be

Fixed costs	$205,000
Variable cost $\dfrac{\$150,000}{200,000 \text{ units}} \times 180,000 \text{ units} =$	135,000
Total cost	$340,000

The new factory costs would be

Fixed costs	$178,000
Variable cost $\dfrac{\$180,000}{200,000 \text{ units}} \times 180,000 \text{ units} =$	162,000
Total cost	$340,000

The new factory would still be preferred because any quantity less than 180,000 units would favor this decision.

(c) At 200,000 units, expansion would cost

Fixed costs	$205,000
Variable cost $\dfrac{\$150,000}{200,000 \text{ units}} \times 200,000 \text{ units} =$	150,000
Total cost	$355,000

The new plant would cost

Fixed costs	$178,000
Variable cost $\dfrac{\$180,000}{200,000 \text{ units}} \times 200,000 \text{ units} =$	180,000
Total cost	$358,000

Therefore, the company should expand its current plant if it expects condition (c) to hold.

3.1. FIFO: 300 ending units @ $3.20 = $960

Periodic LIFO: 300 ending units consist of

200 @ $3.00/unit =	$600
100 @ 3.10/unit =	310
Total	$910

Weighted average: $\dfrac{\text{Total purchases}}{\text{Total units}}$ $\dfrac{\$9,920}{3,200} = \$3.10/\text{unit}$

300 ending units @ $3.10 = $930

3.2. $0 = \sqrt{\dfrac{2PQ}{C}} = \sqrt{\dfrac{2(15)\,(300,000)}{2.25}} = \sqrt{\dfrac{9,000,000}{2.25}}$

$$= \sqrt{4,000,000} = 2,000 = \text{EOQ}$$

4.1.

Salaries		Work in process Materials		Finished goods
(3)1,300	1,300(10)	(4)4,000	3,000(5)	(5)3,000
				(6)5,000
				(9)3,750

Rent			Indirect labor			Work in process Overhead		
(7)2,500	2,500(10)		(8)2,800	2,800(10)		(10)6,600	3,750(9)	

	Cash		Inventory Raw materials			Work in process Direct labor		
	10,000(1)		(1)10,000	4,000(4)		(2)8,000	5,000(6)	
	8,000(2)							
	1,300(3)							
	2,500(7)							
	2,800(8)							

Entry 9 is to absorb overhead on the finished goods (75 percent of $5,000). Entry 10 is to close the overhead accounts to work in process overhead.

Trial Balance

Cash		$24,600
Inventory—raw materials	$ 6,000	
Work in process—direct labor	3,000	
Work in process—overhead (75% of $3,000)	2,250	
Work in process—materials	1,000	
Underabsorbed overhead ($2,850 − 2,250)	600	
Finished goods	11,750	
	$24,600	$24,600

or

Cash		$24,600
Inventory—raw materials	$ 6,000	
Work in process—direct labor	3,000	
Work in process—overhead*	2,475	
Work in process—materials	1,000	
Finished goods	12,125	
	$24,600	$24,600

* The actual overhead rate is 82.5 percent of direct labor.

$$\frac{\$6,600}{\$8,000} = 82.5 \text{ percent}$$

4.2. (a) Journal entries

(1) Work in process—Job 17	$12,600	
Work in process—Job 18	18,450	
Work in process—Job 19	26,000	
Wages payable		57,050
(2) Work in process—Job 17	12,400	
Work in process—Job 18	11,550	
Work in process—Job 19	27,000	
Raw materials control		50,950
(3) Work in process—Job 17	15,000	
Work in process—Job 18	22,500	
Work in process—Job 19	32,500	
Overhead—Applied		70,000
(4) Finished goods	334,000	
Work in process—Job 17		123,000
Work in process—Job 18		114,500
Work in process—Job 19		96,500
Cost of Sales	334,000	
Finished goods		334,000
Accounts receivable	420,000	
Sales		420,000

(b) Gross profit rate $= \dfrac{\text{Sales} - \text{Cost of Sales}}{\text{Sales}}$

Job 17 $\quad \dfrac{180,000 - 123,000}{180,000} = 31.6\%$

Job 18 $\quad \dfrac{140,000 - 114,500}{140,000} = 18.2\%$

Job 19 $\quad \dfrac{100,000 - 96,500}{100,000} = 3.5\%$

5.1. (a) Equivalent units

	Labor and overhead		Materials	
Units beginning work in process	25,000		25,000	
Completion (40%)	10,000	15,000	25,000	0
Units transferred out	105,000		105,000	
Units beginning work in process	25,000	80,000	25,000	80,000
Units ending work in process	20,000		20,000	
Not completed (50%)	10,000	10,000	0	20,000
Equivalent units		105,000		100,000

(b) Value of goods transferred out

Beginning work in process		$60,000
Current period costs		
Transferred in	$135,000	
Materials	55,000	
Labor and overhead	136,500	326,500
Total costs		$386,500

Costs per equivalent units

Transfers in $\dfrac{\$135,000}{100,000} = \$1.35$

Materials added $\dfrac{\$55,000}{100,000} = \$ .55$

Labor and overhead added $\dfrac{\$136,500}{105,000} = \$1.30$

Beginning inventory		$60,000	
Labor and overhead (this period)			
(15,000 equivalent units @ $1.30)		19,500	$79,500
Units completed			
Transfer in costs	(80,000 × $1.35)	$108,000	
Materials	(80,000 × $ .55)	44,000	
Labor and overhead	(80,000 × $1.30)	104,000	256,000
Value of units transferred out			$335,500

(c) Value of closing inventory

Transfer in costs	(20,000 × $1.35)	$27,000	
Materials	(20,000 × $ .55)	11,000	
Labor and overhead	(10,000 × $1.30)	13,000	$51,000

6.1.

	Total	A	B	C
Sale price	$14,550	$3,750	$4,800	$6,000
Incremental costs	4,550	1,250	800	2,500
Sales value, less incremental costs	$10,000	$2,500	$4,000	$3,500
		(25%)	(40%)	(35%)
Costs to split-off point				
Raw materials	$ 2,400			
Processing	3,000			
Total joint costs	5,400	$1,350	$2,160	$1,890
Incremental costs	4,550	1,250	800	2,500
Allocated costs	$ 9,950	$2,600	$2,960	$4,390

6.2. **(a)** Computation of cost of goods manufactured

Cost of materials	$660,000
Cost of labor and overhead	200,000
Total cost of goods manufactured	$860,000

Total market value

C	60% × 10,000 units × $120/unit	= $720,000
D	30% × 10,000 units × $180/unit	= 540,000
F	10% × 10,000 units × $ 30/unit	= 30,000
		$1,290,000

Cost of goods manufactured assigned to

Product C $\dfrac{720,000}{1,290,000}$ × $860,000 = $480,000

Product D $\dfrac{540,000}{1,290,000}$ × $860,000 = 360,000

Product F $\dfrac{30,000}{1,290,000}$ × $860,000 = 20,000

Total $860,000

(b) Computation of cost of goods sold

	Cost of goods mfd. (a)	Units mfd. (b)	Cost/ unit (c)	Units sold (d)	Cost/ units sold (e)
Product C	$480,000	6,000	$ 80	5,000	$400,000
Product D	360,000	3,000	120	2,500	300,000
Product F	20,000	1,000	20	1,000	20,000
	$860,000	10,000		8,500	$720,000

(c) Ending inventory

C	1,000 @	80 =	$ 80,000
D	500 @	120 =	60,000
F	–0–		
	Total		$140,000

7.1. **(a)** Spoiled production excluded
Equivalent units:

Beginning inventory	10,000 units
Started and completed	8,000 units
Ending inventory (.5 × 12,000)	6,000 units
Total equivalent production	24,000 units

Unit cost $\dfrac{\$48,000}{24,000} = \$2.00$

(b) Spoiled production included
Equivalent units:

Beginning inventory	10,000 units
Started and completed	8,000 units
Spoiled production	1,000 units
Ending inventory	6,000 units
Total equivalent production	25,000 units

Unit cost $\dfrac{\$48,000}{25,000} = \$1.92$

8.1. (a) is on p. 244.

8.1. (b) **Service** department allocation to production and service departments:

Dept.	Total	A	M	D	C	I	G
A	100%	—	20%	10%	20%	20%	30%
M	100%	20%	—	10%	20%	30%	20%
D	10%	10%	10%	—	30%	40%	10%

8.2. From this, derive equations:

$A = \$300,000 + .2M + .1D$
$M = \$180,000 + .2A + .1D$
$D = \$100,000 + .1A + .1M$
$C = \$200,000 + .2A + .2M + .3D$
$I = \$150,000 + .2A + .3M + .4D$
$G = \$200,000 + .3A + .2M + .1D$

Solving yields:	C	I	G
Total overhead	377,435	370,897	381,668
Divide by direct-labor hours	20,000	40,000	10,000
Cost per direct-labor hour	$18.87	$9.27	$38.17

8.1. (a)

Single Step Method

	Service Departments			Revenue Departments		
	A	M	D	C	I	G
Costs before allocation	$300,000	$180,000	$100,000	$200,000	$150,000	$200,000
First step:						
Allocate administration costs						
10/50, 5/50, 10/50,						
10/50, 15/50	(300,000)	60,000	30,000	60,000	60,000	90,000
Second step:						
Allocate maintenance costs						
(10/80, 20/80,						
30/80, 20/80)		(240,000)	30,000	60,000	90,000	60,000
Third step:						
Allocate design costs						
3/8, 4/8, 1/8			(160,000)	60,000	80,000	20,000
Totals				$380,000	$380,000	$370,000
Divide by direct-labor hours				20,000	40,000	10,000
Cost per direct-labor hour				$19.00	$9.50	$37.00

9.1.

	JAN.	FEB.	MAR.	APR.	MAY	JUNE	JULY	AUG.	SEPT.	OCT.	NOV.	DEC.
Cash Balance Beginning	30,000	45,000	29,000	29,000	49,000	58,000	88,000	67,000	67,000	46,000	46,000	61,000
RECEIPTS												
Sales 60 days previous	25,000	25,000	40,000	40,000	40,000	40,000	10,000	10,000	10,000	10,000	25,000	25,000
Short-term borrowing		10,000										
Cash available	55,000	80,000	69,000	69,000	89,000	98,000	98,000	77,000	77,000	56,000	71,000	86,000
PAYMENTS												
Materials		21,000			21,000		21,000		21,000			21,000
Wages, and so on	10,000	10,000	10,000	10,000	10,000	10,000	10,000	10,000	10,000	10,000	10,000	10,000
Dividends		20,000										
Taxes			30,000									
Repayment of loans				10,000								
Total payments	10,000	51,000	40,000	20,000	31,000	10,000	31,000	10,000	31,000	10,000	10,000	31,000
BALANCE	45,000	29,000	29,000	49,000	58,000	88,000	67,000	67,000	46,000	46,000	61,000	55,000
MATERIALS (in tons)												
Opening balance	30	60	40	20	50	30	60	40	20	50	30	60
Receipts	50			50		50			50		50	
Subtotal	80	60	40	70	50	80	60	40	70	50	80	60
Used	20	20	20	20	20	20	20	20	20	20	20	20
BALANCE	60	40	20	50	30	60	40	20	50	30	60	40

9.2.　(a)　Budget for 30,000 units

Fixed costs:		
Depreciation	$ 2,000	
Rent	8,000	
Supervisors	7,000	$ 17,000
Variable costs:		
Electricity (30,000) ($.30)	$ 9,000	
Repairs (30,000) ($.10)	3,000	
Maintenance (30,000) ($.25)	7,500	
Wages (30,000) ($6.00)	180,000	
Materials (30,000) ($2.00)	60,000	$259,000
		$276,000

(b)　Budget for 40,000 units
Fixed costs as above

		$ 17,000
Variable costs:		
Electricity (40,000) ($.30)	$ 12,000	
Repairs (40,000) ($.10)	4,000	
Maintenance (40,000) ($.25)	10,000	
Wages (40,000) ($6.00)	240,000	
Materials (40,000) ($2.00)	80,000	$346,000
		$363,000

10.1.　Two-variance method
Total variance computation

Fixed overhead		$ 8,000
Variable overhead		14,000
Total overhead		$22,000

Overhead per unit $22,000/20,000　　　$ 1.10

Fixed $\dfrac{\$8,000}{20,000} = \$.40$

Variable $\dfrac{\$14,000}{20,000} = \$.70$

Standard overhead for units produced 19,500 × $1.10		$21,450
Actual overhead		
Fixed	$ 8,350	
Variable	15,500	$23,850

Budgeted overhead		21,450
Total variance		2,400 U

Noncontrollable variance computation

Budgeted @ 19,500 unit production		
Fixed	$ 8,000	
Variable (19,500 × $.70)	13,650	$21,650
Standard (19,500 × $1.10)		21,450
Noncontrollable variance		$ 200 U

or

500 units (20,000 − 19,500) × $.40 fixed overhead per unit =	$ 200 U

Controllable variance computation

Actual overhead		$23,850
Budgeted @ 19,500 units: fixed	$ 8,000	
variable 19,500 @ $.70	13,650	21,650
Controllable variance		$ 2,200 U

or

Actual variable overhead	$15,500
Budgeted variable overhead	
(19,500 × $.70)	13,650
	$ 1,850 U

Add:

Actual fixed overhead	$ 8,350	
Budgeted fixed overhead	8,000	350 U
Controllable variance		$ 2,200 U

Three-variance method
Efficiency variance

Actual hours (4,200 × $5.50 standard)	$23,100
Budgeted hours for 19,500 units	
(3,900 × $5.50 standard)	21,450
Efficiency variance	$ 1,650 U

Capacity variance

Actual hours		4,200
Normal hours		4,000
Hours worked over normal		200
Fixed overhead rate per hour		$ 2
Capacity variance		$ 400 F

or

Actual hours (4,200 × $5.50)		$23,100
Budgeted overhead @ 4,200 hours		
Fixed	$ 8,000	
Variable (4,200 × $3.50)	14,700	$22,700
Capacity variance		$ 400 F

Budgetary variance

Actual overhead		$23,850
Budgeted @ 4,200 hours		
Fixed	$ 8,000	
Variable (4,200 × $3.50)	14,700	22,700
Budgetary variance		$ 1,150 U

Recapitulation

Efficiency variance	$ 1,650 U
Capacity variance	400 F
Budgetary variance	1,150 U
Total variance	$ 2,400 U

Four-variance method

Spending variance (budgetary variance above)	$1,150 U

Efficiency variance

Budget @ 4,200 hours		
(see computation above)		$22,700
Budget for units produced		
Fixed overhead	$ 8,000	

Variable overhead

(19,500 × $.70)   13,650   21,650

                Total $ 1,050 U

Idle capacity variance (capacity variance above) $ 400 F

Effectiveness variance

Actual hours for 19,500 units	4,200	
Standard hours for 19,500 units	3,900	300 U
Fixed overhead rate per hour		$ 2
Total		$ 600 U

Recapitulation

Spending variance	$ 1,150 U
Efficiency variance	1,050 U
Idle capacity	400 F
Effectiveness	600 U
Total	$ 2,400 U

10.2. Overhead variance

Standard overhead for units produced

$60 \times 800 \times \$2.60 = \$124,800$

Overhead cost   125,000

Overhead variance $ 200* unfavorable
                                                    variance

* Since no breakdown of fixed and variable costs is available, there is no determination of controllable and noncontrollable variance.

Labor variance

Standard labor for units produced

$800 \times \$4 \times 60 = \$192,000$

Actual labor   200,000

Efficiency variance $ 8,000 unfavorable

There is no labor wage variance.

Materials variances

Total variance

$$\begin{array}{ccc} \text{Standard} & \text{standard} & \\ \text{lbs.} & \times & \text{price} & \times \text{production} \end{array}$$

550	×	.60	×	60	=	$ 19,800
Actual cost						15,000

Total variance, $ 4,800 favorable

which is broken down into

Usage variance

Actual quantity at standard price
    30,000 @ $.60 $ 18,000

Standard quantity for units produced
  at standard price
    33,000 @ $.60   19,800

                                                        $ 1,800 favorable

Price variance

Actual quantity × actual rate $ 15,000
Actual quantity × standard rate
    30,000 × .60   18,000

                                                        $ 3,000 favorable

Summary

Standard cost $5,610 ×
    60 batches   = $336,600
Actual cost   340,000

Unfavorable variance $ 3,400

Made up of
    Overhead $ 200 unfavorable
    Labor efficiency   8,000 unfavorable
    Material usage   1,800 favorable
    Material price   3,000 favorable
Net $ 3,400 unfavorable

11.1. See pages 142–144 for graphs.
        Break-even Point

$$\text{BEP} = \frac{\$750,000}{1 - \frac{2}{5}} = \$1,250,000$$

$$BEP = \frac{\$750,000}{\frac{3}{5}} = \$1,250,000$$

Sales needed for a profit of $600,000

$$S = \frac{\$750,000 + \$600,000}{1 - \frac{2}{5}} = \$2,250,000$$

$$\frac{\$2,250,000\,(Sales)}{\$5\,(Unit\ price)} = 450,000\ units$$

Profit on sales of 400,000 units at $6 per unit

Sales = 400,000 units × $6 = $2,400,000

$$2,400,000 = \frac{\$750,000 + Profit}{1 - \frac{2}{6}}$$

Profit = $850,000

11.2.

(a) **Break-even point** $= \dfrac{\text{Fixed cost}}{\text{Sales} - \text{variable costs}} = \dfrac{\$300,000}{\$100 - 70} = $ **10,000 units**

   10,000 units × $100 unit selling price = $1,000,000 break-even point

(b) $\dfrac{\$360,000}{100 - 70} = $ 12,000 units: 12,000 × $100 =

   $1,200,000 break-even point

(c) $\dfrac{\$300,000}{100 - 60} = $ 7,500 units: 7,500 × $100 = $750,000 break-even point

(d) **Required profit** = 15% × $200,000 = $30,000

   $\dfrac{\$300,000 + \$30,000}{\$100 - \$70} = $ 11,000 units: 11,000 × $100 = $1,100,000

12.1. Effect of change in sales mix

	Budget	*Actual*
Product A	3/8	4/9
Product B	5/8	5/9

Product A
mix variance $= [(3/8 \times 90,000) - 40,000] \times \$2.00$
$= \$12,500\ U$

Product B
mix variance $= [(5/8 \times 90,000) - 50,000] \times \$2.00$
$= \$12,500$ F

Mix variance

	Product A	$12,500 U
	Product B	12,500 F
	Total	$ 0

Effect of change in quantity sold

Product A
quantity variance $= [(3/8 \times 90,000) - 30,000] \times \$2.00$
$= \$7,500$ F

Product B
quantity variance $= [(5/8 \times 90,000) - 50,000] \times \$2.00$
$= \$12,500$ F

Quantity variance

$=$	Product A	$ 7,500 F
	Product B	$12,500 F
	Total	$20,000 F

Effect of change in sales price

Product A = ($6.20 − $6.00) × 40,000 =	$ 8,000 F
Product B = ($7.64 − $8.00) × 50,000 =	$18,000 U
Total	$10,000 U

Effect of change in unit cost

Product A = ($4.00 − $4.10) × 40,000 =	$ 4,000 U
Product B = ($6.00 − $5.72) × 50,000 =	14,000 F
Total	$10,000 F

Summary

Sales mix variance	$ 0
Quantity variance	20,000 F
Price variance	10,000 U
Cost variance	10,000 F
Net increase in profit	$20,000 F

12.2.   New standard
             45 R @ $3. = $135
             20 Q @ 2. =   40
             50 T @ 1. =   50
                            $225 for 100–10% = 90 widgets

Cost of good widgets = $\dfrac{225}{90}$ = $2.50 per widget under new
                                                plan

Cost of good widgets = $\dfrac{240}{100}$ = $2.40 under old plan
                                            .10 unfavorable material
                                                variance per good
                                                widget

Explained as
    Mix variance
    R-(60 − 45) × $.03 = $.45 F
    Q-(20 − 20) × .02 = .00
    T-(20 − 50) × .01 = .30 U
                          $.15 F

Yield variance $\dfrac{\$2.25}{.9}$ − $2.25 = $.25 U

13.1. (a) Contribution margin per unit equals sales minus
           variable costs

                        S − VC = CM
                        $99 − $33 = $66

                        EDDY COMPANY
    (b)   DIRECT COSTING INCOME STATEMENT
                     FOR SALES OF 10,000 UNITS

             Sales $990,000
             Less: Variable costs   330,000
             Contribution margin $660,000

Less: Fixed costs

Production	$166,000	
Selling	90,000	
Administrative	142,000	398,000
Net income		$262,000

14.1.

Cost of goods sold		$6,500,000
Depreciation	$300,000	
Taxes, insurance, and so on	500,000	800,000
Net variable costs		$5,700,000
Variable costs per unit		$ 57
Selling price per unit		70
Potential profit per unit		$ 13

Pro forma Operating Statement

	Present	Added	Total
Sales	$10,000,000	$2,800,000	$12,800,000
Variable costs	5,700,000	2,280,000	7,980,000
	$ 4,300,000	$ 520,000	$ 4,820,000
Fixed costs	2,000,000		2,000,000
Contribution margin	$ 2,300,000	$ 520,000	$ 2,820,000

14.2.

	Alternative 1	Alternative 2
Proceeds from immediate sale		
70% × 60% × $40,000	$16,800	
50% × 60% × $40,000, less advertising	($2,000)	$10,000
Additional discounts		
($16,800 − 10,000) × .04 × 12	3,264*	
Additional proceeds from later sales		
50% × 80% × 60% × $40,000		9,600
	$20,064	$19,600

* This figure assumes a constant turnover of inventory, therefore, only simple interest is used.

Alternative 1 is better even without quantifying storage, clerical costs, and risk involved in Alternative 2.

15.1.

$$\frac{2,982}{25,000} = .119280$$

Figure 15.2, Periodic payment to amortize $1 and interest, shows this to be 12 years.

15.2.

$$\frac{7,142}{2,000} = 3.571$$

Figure 15.5, Present value of an annuity of $1, shows the rate of interest to be 25 percent.

15.3. A 7 percent rate of return is not shown in Figure 15.4 or 15.5 but can be interpolated from Figure 15.2.

$$\frac{1}{.167468} = 5.97$$

$5.97 \times 4 = \$23,880.$

16.1.

Current profits — Sales 400,000 @ $3.50		$1,400,000
Less variable costs		
4 × $235,000		940,000
Contribution margin		$ 460,000
Fixed costs		300,000
Current profits		$ 160,000
Desired profit increase =		
50% × $160,000		$ 80,000

Increase in Income		
$.25 × 400,000	$100,000	
Less increase in cost*	10,000	
(10% of increase in income)		
Increase in contribution margin	$ 90,000	
Desired increase in profits	80,000	
Available for advertising	$ 10,000	

* Selling costs that vary in proportion to revenues

$$\frac{\$\ \ 35,000}{\$\ 350,000} = 10\%$$

Revenues per 100,000 boxes at old price

16.2.

	Total	A	B	C	D
Sales	$350,000	$75,000	$125,000	$50,000	$100,000
Cost of product	215,000	45,000	75,000	25,000	70,000
Contribution margin	$135,000	$30,000	$ 50,000	$25,000	$ 30,000
Assigned costs	75,000	20,000[a]	37,500[b]	7,500[c]	10,000[d]
Net income	$ 60,000	$10,000	$ 12,500	$17,500	$ 20,000

(a) $1,000 \times 200 = 200,000 = \dfrac{20}{75}$: $\dfrac{20}{75} \times 75,000 = 20,000$

(b) $2,500 \times 150 = 375,000 = \dfrac{1}{2}$: $\dfrac{1}{2} \times 75,000 = 37,500$

(c) $500 \times 150 = 75,000 = \dfrac{1}{10}$: $\dfrac{1}{10} \times 75,000 = 7,500$

(d) $1,000 \times 100 = 100,000 = \dfrac{10}{75}$: $\dfrac{10}{75} \times 75,000 = 10,000$

Given Department A's display space, Department C might well make a larger proportionate contribution to overall margin because its contribution margin is 50 percent of sales. In fact, any change in the allocation of assigned costs could materially affect the net income of the various products, disguising the importance of the contribution margin.

18.1.

	Total	A	B	C
Contribution margin	$300,000	100,000	100,000	100,000
Profit on sales (gross)	30%	20%	33⅓ %	50%
(net)	5%	<25%>	8.3%	25%
Return on investment (gross)	120%	200%	100%	100%
(net)	20%	<25%>	25%	50%

18.2. (a) If all nidgets produced are sold on the open market,

Sales (20,000 × $300)	$6,000,000
Variable costs (20,000 × $200)	4,000,000
Contribution margin	$2,000,000

However, if nidgets are used to complete widgets,

Sales (20,000 × $400)	$8,000,000
Variable costs [20,000 × (200 + 160)]	7,200,000
Contribution margin	$ 800,000

Obviously, the contribution margin of selling the intermediate product (nidgets) is much larger than that of continuing production and selling widgets. Division F should stop operation.

(b)

	Selling only 14,000 nidgets	Selling 14,000 nidgets and 6,000 widgets
Sales	$4,200,000	$6,600,000
Variable costs	2,800,000	4,960,000
Contribution margin	$1,400,000	$1,640,000

In this case, the company should continue to make and sell 6,000 widgets.

19.1.

$$\text{Contribution margin} = \$6\,A + \$7\,B$$
$$120,000 = 1\,A + 2\,B$$
$$40,000 = A$$
$$50,000 = B$$

Solving algebraically yields

$$A = 40,000 \text{ units}$$
$$B = 40,000 \text{ units}$$
$$\text{Contribution margin} = 40,000(6) + 40,000(7) = \$520,000$$

19.2.

(a) Computation of conditional values (CV) for four (4) preparers

Revenue per 960 returns	$ 19,200
Cost of 4 preparers for 12 weeks	−7,200
CV	$ 12,000

(b) Computation of conditional values for five (5) preparers

Number of returns prepared	960	1,200
Revenues	$19,200	$24,000
Cost of 5 preparers	9,000	9,000
CV	$10,200	$15,000

(c) Computation of conditional values for six (6) preparers

Number of returns prepared	960	1,200	1,440
Revenues	$19,200	$24,000	$28,800
Cost of 6 preparers	10,800	10,800	10,800
CV	$ 8,400	$13,200	$18,000

(d) Computation of conditional values for seven (7) preparers

Number of returns prepared	960	1,200	1,440	1,680
Revenues	$19,200	$24,000	$28,800	$33,600
Cost of 7 preparers	12,600	12,600	12,600	12,600
CV	$ 6,600	$11,400	$16,200	$21,000

Payoff Table

Event	Probability of event	4 Preparers CV	4 Preparers EV	5 Preparers CV	5 Preparers EV	6 Preparers CV	6 Preparers EV	7 Preparers CV	7 Preparers EV
				Possible Actions: Hire					
960 returns	.20	$12,000	$2,400	$10,200	$2,040	$ 8,400	$1,680	$ 6,600	$1,320
1,200 returns	.40	12,000	4,800	15,000	6,000	13,200	5,280	11,400	4,560
1,440 returns	.30	12,000	3,600	15,000	4,500	18,000	5,400	16,200	4,860
1,680 returns	.10	12,000	1,200	15,000	1,500	18,000	1,800	21,000	2,100
	1.00								
Total expected value			$12,000		$14,040		$14,160		$12,840

From this we see that the firm should hire six (6) preparers.

Index